2/2011

Sex, Love, and Mental Illness

SEX, LOVE, AND MENTAL ILLNESS

A Couple's Guide to Staying Connected

Stephanie Buehler

Foreword by Barry W. McCarthy, PhD

Sex, Love, and Psychology
Judy Kuriansky, Series Editor

PRAEGER

AN IMPRINT OF ABC-CLIO, LLC
Santa Barbara, California • Denver, Colorado • Oxford, England

Library of Congress Cataloging-in-Publication Data

Buehler, Stephanie.
 Sex, love, and mental illness : a couple's guide to staying connected / Stephanie Buehler ; foreword by Barry W. McCarthy.
 p. cm.—(Sex, love, and psychology)
 Includes bibliographical references and index.
 ISBN 978-0-313-38686-2 (hard copy : alk. paper)—ISBN 978-0-313-38687-9 (ebook) 1. Mentally ill—Sexual behavior. 2. Couples. 3. Intimacy (Psychology) 4. Sex. I. Title.
 RC455.4.S44B84   2011
 616.89´1562—dc22   2010039771

ISBN: 978-0-313-38686-2
EISBN: 978-0-313-38687-9

15   14   13   12   11   1   2   3   4   5

This book is also available on the World Wide Web as an eBook.
Visit www.abc-clio.com for details.

Praeger
An Imprint of ABC-CLIO, LLC

ABC-CLIO, LLC
130 Cremona Drive, P.O. Box 1911
Santa Barbara, CA 93116-1911

This book is printed on acid-free paper ∞

Manufactured in the United States of America

I dedicate this book first to my husband of 25 years, Mark. Thank you for your patience and support while I wrote this book. I couldn't ask for a better partner.

I also want to acknowledge the special role of my daughter, Anneka, who hopes to follow in my footsteps as a psychologist. Thank you for your help in bringing this book to fruition, and for your patience and support. I couldn't ask for a better daughter.

CONTENTS

SERIES FOREWORD

I am exceptionally proud to have Dr. Stephanie Buehler's important and groundbreaking book in my series and recommend it as essential reading for every mental health professional. When Dr. Buehler first discussed her book idea with me—that she wanted to explain the impact on intimacy of various psychological conditions, particularly those listed in the manual professionals know as the *Diagnostic and Statistical Manual* (DSM)—I was thrilled because I knew how this is an important topic. Her project sparked my enthusiasm and support for reasons that touched on many aspects of my professional experiences over many years. For example, I had spent years answering people's most personal questions in public forums about diverse problems that are in the DSM, from depression to eating disorders, addictions, and attention deficits—all of which Dr. Buehler was going to address from a scholarly perspective that would be readable by professionals as well as by the public. I had also been a senior research scientist years earlier and served on a committee designing the categories of sexual disorders for an early edition of the DSM, as well as working on a cross-cultural diagnostic project concerning patients diagnosed with schizophrenia and depression. As part of that project, at the request of the "grandparents" of sex therapy, Masters and Johnson, my team had done pioneering work on evaluating sexual dysfunction in patient populations. And further, as a sex therapist and as a clinical psychologist who has taught clinical psychology, done recovery work after disasters, and treated many people—in hospital settings and private practice—suffering from many of the conditions listed in the DSM, I knew the importance of the connection between sexuality and psychological states.

I also knew how little is available in the field that makes all the connections Dr. Buehler was proposing. Further, I knew what a major undertaking it would be to tackle the topic.

Now that her book is complete, Dr. Buehler has done a brilliant job on all fronts. She has expertly unraveled the complicated interaction between sexual health and mental health. In each chapter, she details this interaction for different major disorders listed in the DSM, presenting statistics and symptoms, as well as examples of cases. As a psychologist and sex therapist certified by the American Association of Sex Educators, Counselors and Therapists, Dr. Buehler shows in this book that she knows her topic well. Her well-written introduction does an excellent job outlining the richness of the contents and engaging the reader. Each chapter addressing a condition is professionally referenced, giving valuable resources for each disorder as well as for the topic as a whole. Each chapter is also well-organized and brilliantly compacts extensive information, presenting the diagnostic condition in a consistent outline, which helps the processing of information.

The resulting comprehensive and scholarly work is most impressive. I am sure colleagues will feel similarly and find this book highly useful in their practice, research, and teaching.

The general reader can also benefit vastly from reading this book, given its clear descriptions of the conditions, identifiable case examples, and practical suggestions. Especially appealing in this regard are the descriptions of sensate focus exercises and of mindfulness in enriching sexuality and relationships.

Congratulations and thanks to Dr. Buehler for sharing her expertise in such an important resource.

Dr. Judy Kuriansky

FOREWORD

It is a privilege to write the foreword to this groundbreaking book—the first to address issues of couples' therapy, sexuality, and mental illness. Stephanie Buehler is a well-respected psychologist, couples therapist, and sex therapist who has the courage to write in detail about the challenges of different forms of mental illness and their specific impacts on individuals, couples, and sexuality.

Although lay readers will benefit greatly from this book, it is written mainly for clinicians—whether psychologists, psychiatrists, nurses, social workers, ministers, or counselors. The traditional health and mental health professionals do not receive extensive training in couples' therapy, much less assessment and treatment of sexual problems and dysfunctions. This book fills a critical void to help clinicians understand, assess, and treat sexual problems involved with mental illness.

The author does an excellent job of describing a wide range of possible problems, from the mild forms to the most severe mental health issues. She uses clinical examples, guidelines, and describes various medical, psychological, relational, and sexual strategies to address these problems.

A special characteristic of this book is its empathy and respectful approach to the person dealing with the mental illness and the partner. It provides a nonblaming, nonshaming approach. The final chapter, "Love and Mental Illness: Tips for Partners," is particularly valuable and empowering. The clinician can suggest that the client or couple read selected sections or chapters to destigmatize the mental health or sexual problem as well as provide useful guidelines and suggestions to successfully address couples' and sexual problems.

This is a wise book that will help clinicians address couples' and sexual issues as part of a comprehensive treatment for a range of mental health problems, including anxiety, depression, pain, eating disorders, alcoholism and drug abuse, personality disorders, ADHD, and Asperger's syndrome, as well as severe mental illness. I highly recommend reading this book, which encourages clinicians to raise relationship and sexual issues with individuals and couples coping with mental illness.

Barry W. McCarthy, PhD

ABBREVIATIONS

ADD	attention deficit disorder
AD/HD	attention deficit disorder, hyperactivity type
AS	Asperger's syndrome
ASPD	antisocial personality disorder
AvPD	avoidant personality disorder
BDD	body dysmorphic disorder
BPD	borderline personality disorder
CSA	childhood sexual abuse
DE	delayed ejaculation
DPD	dependent personality disorder
ED	erectile dysfunction
GAD	generalized anxiety disorder
HD	hypochondriasis disorder
HPD	histrionic personality disorder
LD	learning disability
NPD	narcissistic personality disorder
OCD	obsessive-compulsive disorder
OCPD	obsessive-compulsive personality disorder
PD	pain disorder; personality disorder
PE	premature ejaculation
PTSD	post-traumatic stress disorder
STD	sexually transmitted disease
STI	sexually transmitted infection

Chapter One

INTRODUCTION

If you are an average person, it is no trouble to find a book, magazine article, or Internet site about sex. But if you have a mental illness, your sex life might not be anything like you hoped, and you might not be able to find any information to help you. As a psychologist trained in sex therapy, that is what I realized when a man with severe bipolar disorder came into my office with his wife, reporting that his mental illness had wreaked havoc on their relationship in and out of the bedroom.

The topic of mental illness is taboo, as is sexuality. Put the two together and you have an area into which very few psychologists or researchers of any kind have ventured. However, I was determined to learn all I could so that I could effectively help people such as the couple I saw. In their case, like many, the male bipolar partner took his medication only intermittently. When he was off medication, he would visit massage parlors and then insult his wife for not meeting his sexual needs. When he sensed that his work was being affected, he would go back on his medication and expect his wife to act loving toward him because he was managing so well. In fact, his wife was reeling, trying to recover from the hurt of his infidelity. Certainly, part of their problem was managing the effects of bipolar disorder, but another part was dealing with common sexual problems that had this unique overlay of mental illness.

If a psychologist is left wondering how best to treat sexual problems in similar couples, one can only imagine what couples themselves in that situation might be dealing with. Sometimes, couples may not even realize that their partner's mental disorder, if and when it is diagnosed, has implications for their sexual relationship. Others may recognize the effect but have no idea about how to address the problem. Because sexuality is one of the most basic and important forms of human expression and attachment, when it is adversely affected by mood, anxiety, and other problems, it can undermine the very relationship the mentally troubled person needs for support.

I have written this book not just for myself, but also for those couples as well as therapists that are struggling with problems of sex, intimacy, and mental illness. In each chapter, I will discuss the common relationship problems that a particular mental disorder causes, its particular sexual effects such as erectile dysfunction or lack of desire, and some practical approaches to making sex better. The goal is to encourage couples to acknowledge the genuine issues that they face, then to work together to have satisfying sexual and emotionally intimate time together. Just as people with a chronic physical illness are encouraged to work around limitations to sexual pleasure, people with common mental and psychological problems should be able to enjoy one of the true pleasures that life offers.

The book is broken into two parts. Part I discusses sexuality in general. I educate readers about what sexuality is and its importance in relationships. I then give a brief overview of anatomy and physiology so that couples are aware of how one's mental state affects one's sexual health and pleasure. Finally, I define the various types of sexual dysfunctions as typically experienced by people of all kinds. In chapter 2, the reader will find information about the challenge of couples that have one, or both, partners struggling with a mental disorder. Readers are encouraged to work together to improve their relationship using the tips provided.

Part II covers most of the major problems described in the DSM. The DSM is the current way in which professionals in the field of mental health classify people with similar symptoms so that they can be studied, understood, and treated. Although some people object to the type of labeling that using the DSM entails, a diagnosis can be helpful not only to professionals, but to sufferers who wish to know how to better manage their mental health.

One of the drawbacks of the DSM is not so much the labeling but the fact that all of the diagnoses are assigned to individuals. Unless one is an eccentric recluse, nearly everyone lives in relationship to others. The DSM does not address relationship issues, primarily because it is a publication by the American Psychiatric Association to help psychiatrists prescribe appropriate medication. However, psychotherapists also depend on the DSM. Learning how various emotional problems affect people in a system, whether it is in a family, at work, or in a marriage or long-term relationship, takes some additional understanding.

The most common psychological issues by far are problems of mood and anxiety, so they are covered first in chapters 3 and 4. Both partners can read these chapters to understand the effects of each on sexual experience and expression. Because mood and anxiety can overlap with so many other problems such as anorexia, pain, and attention deficit disorder (ADD), most couples will benefit from looking at these two chapters for additional guidance and suggestions.

The next three chapters are about those problems that are distinctly biopsychosocial; that is, they affect mind and body and are in turn affected by the social environment, including one's relationships. Chapter 5 covers body-related disorders including pain disorder, hypochondriasis (the belief that one has a disease although all evidence is to the contrary), and body dysmorphic disorder (the belief that a part of one's body is abnormal and unattractive although it appears to others as normal). In chapter 6, eating disorders including anorexia and bulimia are covered. Both of these problems are related to the inability to regulate one's own appetite. This inability generalizes to emotions, relationships, and sexuality, making intimacy a challenge for both partners. Finally, the topic of substance abuse and sexuality is addressed in chapter 7. Alcohol, marijuana, and other prescription and nonprescription drugs have varying effects on one's ability to function sexually, but they also interfere with emotional intimacy. The focus on this chapter is on reclaiming sexuality once sobriety has been attained.

Chapters 8 and 9 cover psychological problems that are long-standing. Chapter 8 covers personality disorders. Although problems with personality, such as narcissism and dependence, are generally seen as individual problems, the fact is that they can significantly affect interpersonal relationships, including sexual relationships. Although research on the sexual effects of personality is sparse, personality problems are so prevalent that including them in this book seemed essential.

Chapter 9 includes information on relationships and ADD, learning disabilities, and Asperger's syndrome, which is a type of social autism. All of these problems are based on symptoms generally present at birth and are not so much cured as managed. For a long-term relationship or marriage to succeed, both partners have to understand how these problems affect communication, problem solving, and so on, as well as sexual function.

Chapter 10 deals with serious mental illness, relationships, and sexuality. Although there is a great deal of stigma attached to illnesses such as schizophrenia and psychosis, as well as a tendency to dehumanize and desexualize people with these conditions, they do become involved in sexual and intimate relationships. The effects on one's sexuality occur on many levels, from sexual self-esteem to medications.

HOW TO USE THIS BOOK

Professionals such as therapists, counselors, pastors, doctors, nurses, and others who work to improve mental health in their patients but have no formal training or background in sexuality will find this book straightforward enough that they will be able to put the information and ideas to use immediately. They should note, however, that I have dispensed with organization that comports with the DSM and instead created categories that better fit daily clinical work. In addition, readers who work in the helping professions should be aware that some pertinent DSM categories are undergoing review and may change. For example, sexual desire and sexual arousal may be combined into one category; Asperger's syndrome may disappear from the new edition of the DSM altogether. I ask the reader to approach the material in the spirit in which it was written, as practical ways to manage sexual and relationship concerns that affect people and their partners.

For other readers, I have written this book to address those specific concerns. Mental illness is, of course, extremely complex, making it impossible to write about all the concerns that couples might face in and out of the bedroom. You should, however, be able to find enough information to begin a constructive dialogue of change within your relationship. Be sure to read the introductory chapters on sexuality and mental health. You may learn an entirely new perspective when you think about these topics in the context of relationship, and it will help you understand my approach in the other chapters.

This book was not written to help anyone diagnose or treat a mental disorder. It is recommended to see a mental health professional such as a psychiatrist, psychologist, or licensed professional counselor to get an accurate diagnosis as well as appropriate treatment, including medications, psychotherapy ("talk therapy"), and education about the disorder. Because knowledge about a disorder is critical to making a relationship work, I have included Web resources at the end of each chapter.

It is possible to be diagnosed with more than one disorder. It is also possible that having one disorder, such as an eating disorder, can cause depression. You may, therefore, wish to read more than the chapter on your disorder alone.

Finally, you may want to consider working with a couples' therapist who is an expert at working with couples in which one partner has a psychological diagnosis and sexual problems. You may ask your psychiatrist or individual psychotherapist for a referral. Or, you may visit the American Association of Sexuality Educators, Counselors, and Therapists (AASECT) Web site at http://www.aasect.org to find a certified sex therapist in your area.

Part I

FOUNDATIONS OF SEXUALITY

Chapter Two

UNDERSTANDING SEXUALITY AND MENTAL AND SEXUAL HEALTH: WHAT'S THE CONNECTION?

Although mental and sexual health are very important to a person's quality of life, they are both areas that are misunderstood and even neglected. Making things even more complex, your mental health affects your sexual health, and your sexual health affects your mental health, and both can affect your intimate relationship. For example, one woman may become depressed and no longer enjoy sexual activities, whereas another woman may stop having orgasms and become depressed.

For the purposes of this book, we will be looking mainly at how mental health affects sexual well being, with the exception of chapter 5 on body-related disorders, which specifically discusses the problem of sexual pain disorders. To understand those effects, this chapter will provide information on human sexuality and how it works.

Human sexuality is a very complex topic. All human beings are sexual beings, meaning that they are born with genitals and chromosomes that identify them as male or female. There are also individuals called "intersex" who may have genitals or chromosomes that do not fit into an "either male or female" category. What also makes humans sexual beings is that they have hormones that regulate sexual development and they engage in courting and mating activities for recreation, and for heterosexual couples, procreation. Our sexuality is what drives us to pair with someone for those activities.

For example, your sexual development from infancy to adulthood is dependent on many factors, including those that are biological or physical; social, including family, peers, religion, and culture; and psychological, meaning you as an individual with your own personality, perception, and experiences.

YOUR BIOPSYCHOSOCIAL SEXUALITY

Who we become sexually is as individual as our personalities. Here are some examples of how "biopsychosocial" factors affect human sexual development.

- Biological
  - Girls and boys who enter puberty at a relatively early age may be rushed into sexual activity for which they are emotionally or mentally unprepared.
  - In men, production of the male hormone testosterone peaks around age 35 and then declines gradually beginning at around age 30.
  - In women, progesterone is responsible for regulating the menstrual cycle, which is also part of a woman's sexuality.
- Family
  - Attitudes differ toward sexual curiosity and masturbation.
  - Communication about sex may be open, limited, or avoided.
  - Some parents permit early dating behaviors, whereas others prohibit it.
- Religion
  - May have strict prohibitions against masturbation, premarital sex, and birth control.
  - May suppress any expression of homosexuality.
  - May openly provide sex education and encourage individuals to decide for themselves when to become sexually active.
- Culture
  - Breast enhancement is the most popular plastic surgery in the United States.
  - People believe such sexual myths as "men want sex more than women" and "older adults stop having sex."

Another way to think about sexual development is that there are factors that are contributed from nature (those factors that are biological), nurture (those factors that are social), or a combination of the two. An example of nature might be that learning disabilities may cause someone to lag behind in social skills or have trouble interpreting the words and actions of others. Such problems might interfere with a person's ability to become involved in romantic or sexual relationships in their teens or adulthood. The same outcome—difficulty forming a romantic relationship—can also be due to nurture, as when someone who is emotionally, physically, or sexually abused shuts down feelings and finds it difficult to love.

Some individuals face obstacles in sexual development because of psychological problems present from a young age. For example, a boy who is shy and socially anxious may find it difficult to express emotional feelings or sexual wants or desires as he grows into adolescence and adulthood. A girl who is overly concerned with cleanliness may find herself disgusted by her own body when her vagina produces its natural lubrication. She may become turned off to all bodily functions and fluids, making sex distasteful and the formation of intimate relationships difficult.

Other people have normal, pleasurable sexual experiences until they develop a mental illness. A soldier who returns from combat with post-traumatic stress disorder may no longer have any interest in having sex with his wife or long-term partner. A woman may develop major depression after giving birth to her child (also known as postpartum depression) or have a psychotic episode that leaves her exhausted and emotionally confused even after treatment. It may take more time than either partner would like for her to recover all of her functioning, including interest and participation in sexual activities.

SEXUAL DISORDERS AND MENTAL ILLNESS

Mental and sexual health are intimately entwined, but in complex ways. It may surprise you to learn that sexual problems are included in the DSM, which is the book that mental health professionals use to diagnosis psychological issues. For example, anorgasmia, or lack of orgasm, is a mental disorder. Although there may be medical reasons that a person might not be able to reach orgasm, such as hormone imbalances or damage to the genitals, there are also many psychological reasons that a person might have difficulty experiencing orgasm, including inhibitions or negative thoughts about sex. Although not every woman is bothered by lack of orgasm, for those women who are upset, the condition can have a negative impact on their mental well being.

What the DSM does not cover are the ways in which other, overlapping mental illnesses can contribute to sexual problems. However, although mental illness can affect sexual development, it is also possible for someone with a mental illness to function sexually without much difficulty. For example, many men with attention deficit disorder (ADD) have no problem at all with arousal, erection, or orgasm, whereas for others the hallmark difficulty with mental focus makes sex a struggle. People who are depressed sometimes find that sex is one of the only activities that comforts them or improves their mood, whereas for others sex is the last thing on their minds. Most people who were sexually abused as children are able to enjoy sex as adults.[1]

SEX IS NEEDED FOR GOOD MENTAL HEALTH

Being able to express one's sexuality, whether one is alone or in a relationship, is one of the great joys of life. Sexual behaviors encompass a whole range of activities, from holding hands and cuddling to erotic massage and intercourse. Most loving couples believe that to be as intimate as possible, sexual activity needs to be part of their relationship; without sex, those same couples would say that they feel like roommates or friends. Sex is the way that adults play with one another, the way in which they demonstrate emotions, and a way to create a feeling of trust and attachment.

Can sex be helpful for a person with mental illness? Yes! Being able to function sexually makes most people feel like a "normal" man or woman. Additionally, sexual activity and orgasm can give the brain a boost of serotonin, dopamine, oxytocin (the "cuddle chemical"), and endorphins. Sex can oxygenate the bloodstream and the brain. It can relax muscles and ease headaches and other pains. Sexual activity also helps with hormonal balance, which can be important to brain and mental health. It is a great stress reliever, which is important for overall mental, physical, and emotional health. In addition to all of that, sex simply feels good.

WHAT MAKES SEX SATISFYING?

Contrary to what magazine covers scream out from newsstands or blogs promise on the Internet, satisfying sex only partially involves good love-making technique. The aim of satisfying sex is not to have screaming orgasms (although if you have them, enjoy!), but to feel connected and safe, to trust one's partner with sexual wishes and fantasies, to explore one's body and that of one's partner, and for most people to experience sexual release through orgasm. The expectation should be on having a good sexual experience most of the time, with the understanding that some sexual experiences may be amazing and some just okay.

Almost all couples, not just those in which one or both partners are challenged with a mental illness such as depression or anxiety, go through periods in which there is relatively little sexual activity. Such times might occur during or after major life transitions such as the birth of a child or the death of a parent; a separation, as for work; or an illness or surgery. However, although couples may not want to engage in vigorous sex that includes intercourse, they can still maintain an intimate connection through so-called "outercourse" activities such as holding hands, giving each other foot and neck rubs, full body massage, hugging, cuddling together, spooning, kissing, and manual and oral sex. These activities also count as "sex."

If you are reading this book, it is probably because you want to make a change in your sexual relationship with your partner. Change is made most directly with clear communication between partners. But for many people, communication about sex is especially tricky. In part, that is because we are not really taught how to talk about sex except in ways we learned from peers on the schoolyard or during sleepovers.

In general, you want to clearly identify the problem that you are experiencing. You might even wish to write the problem down so that you can practice saying it aloud to your partner. Let your partner know that you have something that you would like to discuss. Pick a neutral time and place to have your conversation. You might want to start with an observation, such as, "I notice that you haven't been interested in sex," or "Now that you're doing better, I'm finding myself wanting to re connect with you physically. Is that something that interests you, too?"

Let your partner also know that learning to cope better and getting symptoms under control has been a top priority that you support. Tell them that you think the time is right to address the sexual needs that you have. Then listen to your partner. Is he or she ready to be emotionally and physically intimate, and if so, to what degree? Use the information from this book as a guideline to move forward when you and your partner have agreed to be intimate.

What if your partner becomes defensive or declines to discuss the problem at all? Or what if they are not ready to become intimate with you? Try to understand your partner's feelings about the topic. If necessary, seek help from a sex therapist, which is a mental health professional with special training in human sexuality and relationships. You can find a sex therapist through the American Association of Sexuality Educators, Counselors, and Therapists (AASECT) at http://www.aasect.org.

COMMON SEXUAL PROBLEMS

Estimates are that roughly one-fourth of the adult population may have a sexual dysfunction disorder. More women than men report having sexual problems, but that may be because women are more willing to seek help with sexual problems than are men.

The causes of sexual dysfunction disorders are varied, as are their symptoms. In general, symptoms prevent the initiation of sex or the completion of the sex act, or they interfere with satisfaction derived from sex. Almost everyone has some problem with sexual functioning or fulfillment at some point in their lives, but not all problems are considered sexual dysfunction disorders. Sexual satisfaction is highly individual, so what may be a major problem for one couple may be a minor problem for another.

Common types of sexual problems are presented in this chapter for reference as they are discussed throughout the book in conjunction with various mental disorders. Mental illness can be a cause and an effect of sexual problems. For example, a man with depression may develop erectile dysfunction; however, erectile dysfunction that does not have its source in mental issues can cause problems with mood. Worrying about pleasing one's partner instead of enjoying sex can result in performance anxiety, but very often the person who is worried has a pre existing problem with generalized anxiety.

Lack of Sexual Desire

Hypoactive sexual desire (HSD) is a common sexual problem. In couples, it is said to occur when one partner does not initiate sex or does not respond to the initiation of sex. In addition to such mental health problems as depression and anxiety, HSD can be caused by stress, fatigue, such illnesses as diabetes and cancer, hormonal imbalances (especially testosterone), and such relationship concerns as lack of intimacy or trust. Other sexual problems, including sexual pain disorders or lack of orgasm, can also lead to lack of interest in sex. Medications, including antidepressants and oral contraceptives, can also cause HSD. Pregnancy, breastfeeding, and menopause can all interfere with sexual desire.

However, sometimes the higher-desire partner tells the other partner that he or she has low desire, when in fact this is not true. Levels of desire can be mismatched, and a couple may have trouble negotiating how often to have sex. In addition, in long-term relationships it is natural for sexual interest to diminish over time. Such couples need to know how to stimulate interest for themselves and in their partner to prevent sexual boredom.

Lack of Orgasm

Men and women can experience anorgasmia, or lack of orgasm. In men, the condition is also called delayed ejaculation and is rare. For women, anorgasmia is a common problem, affecting approximately one in five women worldwide. Anorgasmia is diagnosed when someone is unable to have orgasm, and in a man's case, ejaculate, even with ample sexual stimulation. To be diagnosed, the DSM states that the condition must also cause personal distress, as there are some people who are not bothered by anorgasmia. Also, it must be the person with anorgasmia who is distressed, not the person's partner.

There are three types of anorgasmia. For the person experiencing primary anorgasmia, orgasm has never occurred. The individual experiencing secondary anorgasmia once had orgasms but now cannot. In situational anorgasmia, the person can only have orgasms under certain conditions. Anorgasmia can be caused by such medical conditions as diabetes and multiple sclerosis; surgeries to the genitals and surrounding areas; medications, especially selective serotonin reuptake inhibitor (SSRI) antidepressants; alcohol and street drug use; menopause; male aging, or andropause; stress; performance anxiety; religious or cultural beliefs; fear of pregnancy or sexually transmitted diseases; and relationship problems, including chronic disagreements, lack of intimate connection, poor communication about sex, and issues related to trust. In men, long-term use of Internet and other pornography can also dampen sexual interest with one's real partner, leading to delayed ejaculation.

Sexual Aversion

Sexual aversion is diagnosed when a person experiences revulsion, disgust, or related emotions when they engage in sexual behavior with a partner. The aversion may be related to certain aspects of sex, such as seeing a partner's genitals, the scent of bodily secretions, or such mild activities as kissing and hugging. Some people are fine with all kinds of sexual activity except for sexual intercourse, which they consequently avoid. Symptoms can range from mild, such as lack of interest and mild disgust, to severe, such as those associated with panic attacks (e.g., shortness of breath, rapid heartbeat, and intense fear).

Causes of sexual aversion include relationship problems (e.g., the discovery of an affair), domestic violence, unresolved disagreements, and lack of hygiene on the part of a partner. Traumatic experiences such as molestation, date rape, or sexual assault can also associate sex with a painful experience that is to be avoided. Finally, religious or cultural teachings can cause sex to be associated with excessive feelings of guilt.

Sexual Pain Disorders

Sex can be physically painful for some people, most of whom are women. At one time, sexual pain was thought to be completely psychological, but it is now understood better as a chronic pain condition in which there is no visible inflammation or injury but the nerves fail to turn off the pain signal to the brain nonetheless. Sexual pain diagnoses include vaginismus, in which the outer part of the vagina spasms, making penetration painful or impossible; vulvodynia, in which the vulva, or exterior area of the female genitals, is affected; and dyspareunia, or pain with intercourse that can occur for women or men. Please be aware that sexual medicine is in its infancy and that you may see other names or terms for these disorders. For example, vaginismus has recently been called "hypertonic pelvic floor dysfunction."

For a woman who has sexual pain, seeking out a physician who has experience with such disorders is critical. Treatment may include topical agents for numbing pain, antidepressant and/or pain medications, dilator therapy, physical therapy with a therapist specializing in pelvic pain, and in some cases surgery. A psychologist or other mental health professional who specializes in pain disorders can also be a beneficial member of the treatment team by helping the woman to cope with pain and its triggers. Counseling sessions can also help a couple be sexual with one another despite the pain disorder. More about each type of disorder is described in chapter 5.

Erectile Dysfunction

Erectile dysfunction (ED) is diagnosed when a man cannot attain or maintain an erection firm enough for sexual activity. Although most men will have such a problem from time to time, when it is a regular occurrence, it can be distressing to the man and his partner. ED is caused by many factors, including psychological problems like depression, performance anxiety, stress, and fatigue; such relationship problems as unresolved discord and infidelity; medical problems including diabetes, obesity, prostate problems, and heart disease; such medications as SSRI antidepressants, medications for high blood pressure, and chemotherapy; such hormonal imbalances as low testosterone or pituitary problems; and heavy or chronic alcohol, tobacco, and marijuana use.

Premature Ejaculation

Premature, or rapid, ejaculation is diagnosed when a man is unable to control how long sexual activity will occur before he has orgasm and ejaculates. Occasional premature ejaculation (PE) is very common, but when it happens on a regular basis, it can become distressing for a man and his partner. The International Society for Sexual Medicine defines PE as not being able to last for more than one minute of intercourse; the normal range is from two to 10 minutes of intercourse.

Like other sexual problems, PE has multiple potential causes. One factor is that early in life, a man may have learned to ejaculate quickly to avoid detection, or to rush through sex because of feelings of guilt. Anxiety, due to fears about one's sexual performance or other, unrelated reasons such as work problems or troubles with extended family, can also contribute to PE. Men who have ED sometimes develop PE. Relationship problems may be a cause, especially if a man has had previously satisfying sexual encounters.

Biological causes of PE include hormone imbalances, certain thyroid problems, an abnormal ejaculatory reflex, inflammation of the prostate or urethra, or even genetics. A medical concern about one's body (e.g., heart health) may cause a man to ejaculate quickly due to what is known as "health anxiety." Stress can also create muscle tension that leads to rapid ejaculation.

NOTE

1. People sexually abused as children may have normal sexual function as adults for many years, but sometimes certain "triggers" may make sex difficult, even if with a long-term partner. Triggers include major life changes such as moving or the birth of a child.

GENERAL RESOURCES ON SEXUALITY

Books

Foley, Sallie, Sally A. Kope, and Dennis P. Sugrue. *Sex Matters for Women: A Complete Guide to Taking Care of Your Sexual Self.* New York: The Guilford Press, 2002.

Joanides, Paul. *The Guide to Getting It On: A New and Mostly Wonderful Book About Sex for Adults for All Ages.* Waldport, OR: Goofy Foot Press, 1998.

McCarthy, Barry W., and Michael E. Metz. *Men's Sexual Health: Fitness for Satisfying Sex.* New York: Routledge, 2007.

Schnarch, David. *Passionate Marriage: Keeping Love and Intimacy Alive in Committed Relationships.* New York: W. W. Norton, 1997.

Online Resources

American Association for Sexuality Educators, Counselors, and Therapists: http://www.aasect.org/.

The Kinsey Institute: http://www.kinseyinstitute.org.

The Sexual Health Network: http://sexualhealth.com.

GENERAL RESOURCES ON MENTAL HEALTH

Online Resources

American Psychiatric Association: http://www.psych.org.

American Psychological Association: http://www.apa.org.

Mayo Clinic: http://www.mayoclinic.com.

MedlinePlus: http://medlineplus.gov.

National Alliance on Mental Illness: http://www.nami.org.

NetWellness: http://netwellness.com.

WebMD: http://www.webmd.com.

Part II

SEXUALITY, PSYCHOLOGY, AND RELATIONSHIPS

Chapter Three

MOOD DISORDERS

DEPRESSION

According to the National Institutes of Mental Health (NIMH), mood disorders are the most common mental health problem in the United States, with nearly 10 percent of adults having a diagnosis of depression, dysthymia (chronic, mild depression), or bipolar disorder in a given year. These three mood disorders not only cause problems with sexual functioning, but the medications used to manage them can also be culprits. Conversely, sexual problems like pelvic pain disorders, rapid (premature) ejaculation, erectile dysfunction (ED), and lack of orgasm can contribute to mood. In fact, sometimes it is difficult to know what happened first: the sexual problem or the mood problem. Either way, mood disorders can interfere with the sex life of the depressed person and the person who loves him or her.

Major depression affects approximately 14.8 million American adults, or 6.7 percent of the population, in a given year, with an average age of onset at 32.5 years of age. It is the leading cause of all disability in the United States for ages 15–44.3 and is more prevalent in women than men. In terms of the sexual effects of depression, one study of 132 patients reported that 72 percent with unipolar depression and 77 percent with bipolar depression expressed a loss of sexual interest or libido (drive).

Dysthymia

Dysthymia is a mood disorder that is best described as a low-grade, chronic form of depression, affecting approximately 3.3 million Americans. For a

WHAT CAUSES DEPRESSION?

Although researchers have made great strides in understanding depression, no one is yet certain of the exact cause. Some research points to biological changes, such as in brain structures like the hippocampus (site of memory); in brain chemistry, such as a decrease in serotonin; and in genetics, because depression seems to run in families. Certain illnesses such as diabetes and multiple sclerosis also seem to be associated with depression, as are some medicines such as beta blockers. From a psychological or social standpoint, grief and loss, interpersonal conflict, and major changes such as job loss, college graduation, or the birth of a child may also bring a depressed mood. Finally, people who abuse such substances as alcohol often have an underlying—and undiagnosed—problem with depression.

diagnosis of dysthymia, a person needs to have only two, rather than six, symptoms of depression. The person also needs to feel a sad or depressed mood for most days over the prior two years or longer. People who have dysthymia are more at risk for an episode of major depression than the overall population.

SYMPTOMS OF DEPRESSION AND DYSTHYMIA

The symptoms of depression and dysthymia are the same, but the number and degree of subjective experience differs between the two disorders. Symptoms include:

- Depressed mood most of the day, nearly every day, as indicated by either subjective report (e.g., feels sad or empty) or observation made by others (e.g., appears tearful). (In children and adolescents, this may be characterized as an irritable mood.)
- Markedly diminished interest or pleasure in all, or almost all, activities most of the day, nearly every day.
- Significant weight loss when not dieting or weight gain (e.g., a change of more than five pounds of body weight in a month), or decrease or increase in appetite nearly every day.
- Insomnia or hypersomnia nearly every day.
- Psychomotor agitation or retardation nearly every day.
- Fatigue or loss of energy nearly every day.
- Feelings of worthlessness or excessive or inappropriate guilt nearly every day.
- Diminished ability to think or concentrate, or indecisiveness, nearly every day.
- Recurrent thoughts of death (not just fear of dying), recurrent suicidal ideation without a specific plan, or a suicide attempt or a specific plan for committing suicide.

For a diagnosis of dysthymia, a person needs to have only two, rather than six, symptoms of depression. The person also needs to feel a sad or depressed mood for most days over the prior two years or longer. People who have dysthymia are more at risk for an episode of major depression than the overall population.

Often, the dysthymic person cannot really say when he or she first began feeling depressed. They may come to think that "the blues" are just part of their nature or personality. It may be that only when they become more depressed and never fully recover that they recognize something is wrong. They also may realize they have dysthymia when they figure out that their "blues" are more long-lasting and a bit more "blue" than what most other people experience.

One symptom of depression is anhedonia, or a lack of pleasure in things that were once enjoyable; sex is often one of those activities in which a person loses interest. Add to that fatigue, lethargy, and a tendency to want to be alone and there are plenty of reasons for depressed persons and their partners to experience a decline in their sex life.

In addition, the medications for treating depression can bring relief as well as sexual side effects, including loss of libido or drive, ED, and lack of or difficulty with orgasm. Consequently, a person treated for depression may have difficulty fulfilling the role of lover and sex partner. The guilt that comes from being unable to fill these roles may have a boomerang effect, in which interest in sex is further lowered.

Depression often goes unrecognized, which also causes problems in the bedroom and elsewhere in the relationship. Also, fears about medication side effects, whether true or untrue, prevent many people from using anti-depressants as part of their treatment. Living with a person who suffers from depression can be challenging in its own right. People living with a person who is depressed can become lonely and sad themselves; it is not unusual for both partners to eventually become depressed. In some cases, in marriages in which there is very little sexual activity, one or both partners are suffering from depression.

And, as stated, sexual dysfunction can cause feelings of sadness, loss of self-worth, hopelessness, and helplessness. For example, a man with ED who is having trouble addressing his problem may come to feel hopeless and depressed. A woman whose husband is disappointed in her lack of sexual pleasure and orgasm may also feel bad.

Earl and Gina

Earl and Gina are both in their late 40s; this is a second marriage for both of them. One of the things that Gina most treasured about Earl was his skill as a lover. She had never experienced anyone so passionate and eager to please her. Earl was also happy to find someone who liked good sex.

But over the past year or so, Earl became less and less passionate. At first, Gina figured that some of the original zing had naturally disappeared, so she suggested a weekend away at their favorite romantic bed and breakfast. Although Earl agreed, he was not much of a companion on the drive up. He only had energy for one round of lovemaking.

Gina sensed that Earl was upset about a recent weak performance review at work, but Earl denied that anything was bothering him. When he got a smaller than expected raise, he became more withdrawn. Try as she might, Gina could not get Earl to open up and talk about his feelings. Their sex life continued to dwindle over the months, as did Earl's zest for any kind of fun. Gina began to wonder if he was not just tired of being married.

Men who are depressed like Earl often have difficulty acknowledging or expressing what they are experiencing. Men are expected to be strong and to focus on thoughts and actions rather than feelings, so they are less likely than women to admit depression. For men, depression is often acted out through their behavior, including low sex drive, social withdrawal and silence, anger or even rage, and substance abuse or other impulsive behaviors.

Men and women who are depressed often complain of fatigue. They feel they lack the energy to work or play, which includes sex. Because people who are depressed may also have low self-esteem, they may feel that they are poor sexual partners. If they have had a change in appetite, a common symptom, they may gain or lose weight, and bad feelings about their body can cause them to avoid sex.

Depression can cause people of both sexes to feel short-tempered. They may become agitated and have a difficult time relaxing. These feelings make experiencing romance tough. They also can have trouble focusing on much of anything, including lovemaking. This can have the effect of pushing a partner away, which only makes the depressed person feel more isolated or inadequate as a partner.

Marilyn

Marilyn has struggled with depression for years. She feels blessed because she has a good marriage and a job she enjoys, a wonderful counterbalance to the hardships she experienced in childhood. As Marilyn advanced in her career, her feelings of doubt and inadequacy began to hound her so that she began to have trouble sleeping and getting motivated to get up in the morning. Marilyn spoke to her doctor. Aware of her struggle, the doctor recommended Paxil, a selective serotonin reuptake inhibitor (SSRI) antidepressant. After a few weeks, Marilyn's mood lifted; in fact, she felt better than ever. However, over time she noticed her orgasms becoming less intense until, ultimately, she stopped having orgasms altogether. Back she went to the physician, who lowered her dose but told her she might have to switch medication if she did not notice an improvement.

Karen and Joe

Karen and Joe went through several attempts at in vitro fertilization before they conceived their first child. Karen was thrilled to become a new mother, but definitely recognized the "baby blues" during the first few weeks postpartum. Although she tried to function to take care of herself and her newborn, the combination of lack of sleep, hormonal adjustment, and money troubles took Karen deeper into depression than the blues. Her gynecologist recommended an antidepressant, which Karen took willingly.

Because of the depression, Karen and Joe did not reconnect sexually until several months after the birth of their son. It took Karen a very long time to have orgasm. When she complained to the doctor, she was switched to another antidepressant, only to have the same result. Two more tries, but Karen's orgasm only seemed more and more frustrating.

Joe could not help but feel unhappy that Karen seemed to continue losing interest in sex, especially when all of her energy seemed to be going into raising their son. Joe tried to be patient, to tell himself that his adult needs came after his little boy's, but he was left feeling lonely, stressed, and sad—and in danger of experiencing his own depression. Seeing a couples' therapist that specialized in sexual issues was helpful to them both.

It is unfortunate but true: Antidepressant medications can cause sexual side effects. These side effects include lack of orgasm, delayed orgasm, difficulty becoming aroused, and low sex drive; in men, medications can cause ED. For many people, switching medications or adding another (see "Sexual Solutions When the Problem Is Depression") can return normal sexual function, as it did for Marilyn. But not everyone is so fortunate.

Janice and Tom

Janice could not remember the last time she felt like having sex. She also rarely felt like going out to see friends, instead staying home to watch a movie and eat ice cream. Tom, her boyfriend of two years, felt that there was something wrong with Janice, but he could not quite put his finger on it. Although Janice tried to enjoy sex when she was with Tom, she found herself apathetic. When she mentioned her low sex drive to her physician at her next checkup, he recommended psychotherapy to help her cope with her blue mood and lack of drive.

Although the idea surprised Janice, she set up an appointment. The therapist encouraged her to exercise and eat a more healthful diet. Janice also learned to monitor her thoughts, discovering that they were more negative than she realized. After several months of therapy, Janice found herself more willing to go out and to be more enthusiastic in bed, although she often felt she had to fight a bit to stand her ground and maintain a more upbeat mood.

If dysthymia is causing you or your partner to have a low sex drive or other sexual problems, then you may find that you really have to consciously work on the underlying mood disorder to optimize your sex life.

* * *

Sexual Solutions When the Problem Is Depression

Many studies have suggested that the treatment of choice for major depression is medication plus psychotherapy, especially cognitive behavioral therapy

(CBT). For people with dysthymia, medication has not been found to be especially helpful, but CBT can be helpful.

CBT can help a depressed person recognize negative thoughts and counter them with ones that are realistic or more positive. Ideally, a depressed person who needs treatment will see a physician or psychiatrist for medication and a psychotherapist for psychotherapy.

This makes perfect sense in the initial stages of diagnosis and treatment of depression. Depression can be lethal if left untreated, so assessing the person with the complaint and ensuring that a plan is in place to decrease symptoms of depression as quickly as possible is a must.

However, when the depression begins to lift, then other problems, such as a person's relationships and sex life, can be addressed. If your treatment provider has not asked you about your love and sex life, then you may need to be the one who brings it to their attention. If you are having a hard time getting your "engine" restarted to feel sexual again or believe your medications are interfering with sexual function, you must speak up, because the most current research suggests that sexual problems caused by antidepressants can become permanent. Although it may be hugely embarrassing, there is no reason to hide from the professionals who are treating you the fact that you are having struggles in the bedroom.

In addition, there is research that demonstrates that sexual activity and orgasm may help ease depression. When a person has orgasm alone or with a partner, it gives a boost to serotonin (a neurotransmitter that scientists think may contribute to a depressed mood when it is low) and raises endorphins and opioids, the brain's so-called "happy chemicals." Orgasm can also help a person relax and fall asleep. It can reawaken a sense of optimism about the future because sex becomes a pleasurable activity to look forward to rather than something to avoid.

Reconnecting after Depression

There are many ways depression can build a wall between two people. The person who is depressed can withdraw or be irritable. He or she can also have negative thoughts about one's self, one's body image, and even one's partner.

If depression goes on for a long time, as it can with postpartum depression or depression that someone is trying to treat without medication, it can be distressing to the well partner. Intentionally or not, they may find themselves angry with the depressed partner for taking away pleasure. They may also be frustrated with the fact that the depressed person may have had more control over how often they have had sex.

Because most couples are uncomfortable talking about sex, tension around the topic can develop. Sex, not depression, can be the new elephant in the room, even after treatment is underway.

The depressed partner may need to establish a sense of compassion for the partner who still has a sex drive. Although the depressed partner may not feel much like re establishing a sexual connection, there are the feelings of one's partner to consider. The depressed partner can become more sexual not out of guilt or pity, but out of love and a wish to show caring.

CHANGING THOUGHTS ABOUT SEX

When it comes to depression, cognitive therapy that helps manage negative thoughts can be helpful. Neutral or positive thoughts about sex can also be developed so that the depressed person has a new outlook on sex. Positive thoughts include that sex:

- Feels good
- Is something to do for one's self as well as one's partner
- Can help lift one's mood
- Can help with relaxation and sleep

Several low-key activities can be used to help couples ease back into being sexual again. For couples whose sex lives have been AWOL, you can start with a modified version of Masters and Johnson's well-known sensate focus activities. Begin with something as gentle as a hand or foot massage. Use lotion or massage oil if you wish. Take turns and be sure not to pressure the depressed partner into going any further than her or his comfort allows. In fact, it is best to create an understanding that for several weeks you are not going to attempt intercourse, just work on getting warmed up to each other again. This understanding builds trust.

From hand or foot massage, you can move on to massaging each other's legs and arms. Once you are comfortable with that, try back massage, too. Try doing all of these exercises fully clothed, or with just a little clothing on (for instance, shorts and a tank top). By this time, you should hopefully be feeling a bit more sensual and can move on to lovemaking or, if not yet prepared for that, mutual manual or oral sex play.

Other ways to create intimacy come from Eastern sexual practices that can be soothing and romantic. You can sit facing one another cross-legged on the bed or another comfortable place. Hold hands, look into each other's eyes, and breathe in synch slowly and gently. If it is too hard to look into each other's eyes, then look at the "third eye," the space on the forehead between the two eyes, or into your partner's left eye only.

Likewise, "spooning," or lying on your sides cupped together with one partner's back against the other's chest, can also be a very nonthreatening way to feel close. Try breathing in synch with one another, then try breathing in an opposite way: When one partner inhales, the other exhales. Switch positions, too, so that each partner has a chance to be held.

Another way to reconnect is to simply explore one another with a single finger. Recline or sit with one another side by side and take turns or mutually touch each other's bodies. Make rules together about what is okay and not okay to touch during these reconnecting sessions.

It may be that the partner with depression may have difficulty becoming aroused or having orgasm. Some people are offended when a lover suggests a vibrator to help things along. But when it feels like too much work to have orgasm, a vibrator can help a person get turned on and have a climax.

Likewise, the nondepressed partner may use the vibrator when the depressed partner lacks energy for intercourse. Women can use a vibrator to explore their inner thighs, mons, labia, clitoris, and vagina. Men can use a vibrator on their inner thighs, testicles, and the underside of the penis.

Establishing a schedule for lovemaking may seem unromantic, but many couples find that doing so takes off some of the pressure of the "will we, won't we make love tonight" dance of uncertainty. Looking together at a calendar can help couples find time for sex.

What if there are many other responsibilities that make having a sex life difficult? Certainly it is fair to seek respite from work or children. Making time for a weekend or a week away is a tried but true "cure" for low drive. Having an opportunity to relax and spend some intimate time together alone can really help couples to be sexual again.

Depression, Sexuality, and Antidepressants

If you do an Internet search on depression and sexuality, you'll see that most of the hits are for sites that talk about the sexual side effects of medication. Of course, it is possible that once you take medications, your mood will lift and your sex life will be fine. That is definitely true for many people. But the fact is that medication can cause sexual dysfunction, including ED, delayed or inhibited orgasm, anorgasmia (no orgasm), and loss of sexual interest (drive or libido).

One of the problems with understanding the sexual side effects of antidepressants is that sexual problems are fairly common in the general population. One large study suggested that as many as 43 percent of women and 35 percent of men will have a sexual problem over the course of their lifetime. However, statistically speaking, people who take antidepressant medication are more at risk than people in the nonpsychiatric population.

Scientists involved in the development of SSRIs hoped that they would be able to avoid sexual side effects with the new medication. In clinical trials, the SSRIs looked promising. However, when prescribed to the population at large, reports of sexual side effects by patients were more than expected.

Why does this happen? Scientists are not certain. Some think that antidepressants are sedating, so they calm the nervous system enough that sexual sensation is dulled. Others believe that antidepressants affect the part of the brain responsible for sexual response and orgasm. And, of course, it is possible that antidepressants relieve most symptoms of depression except sexual desire and function.

Do some antidepressant medications have fewer sexual side effects than others? Bupropion (Wellbutrin), nefazodone (Serzone), mirtazapine (Remeron), and duloxetine (Cymbalta) appear to be the least likely to cause sexual side effects. These medications are sometimes added on when problems with sexual side effects are reported.

What can be done to prevent or work around sexual side effects? If the effects are mild (e.g., it takes longer to have an orgasm, but not too long), then changing things a bit may be all that is required. But if, for instance, you are a man with ED more often than you can tolerate, you may need to talk about changing medication altogether.

However, many people are hesitant to change their medication if they feel that they are having a good result. Here are some suggestions that you can try before making a switch.

- Wait and see. Sometimes your body will build a tolerance to sexual side effects and your problem may just go away on its own.
- Try lowering the dose. But do not do this on your own. Always talk to your doctor before making any change. Your doctor can tell you exactly how to cut back to avoid other side effects such as headache.
- Try having sex before you take your dose of medication.
- Talk to your doctor about adding buproprion (Wellbutrin), mitazapine (Remeron), or bupropion (BuSpar) to counteract sexual side effects.
- Adding a medication designed to treat sexual dysfunction (e.g., Viagra) can remedy ED.

WHICH ANTIDEPRESSANTS CAN CAUSE SEXUAL SIDE EFFECTS?

Studies have demonstrated that the following antidepressants may cause sexual side effects:

- Fluoxetine (Prozac)
- Paroxetine (Paxil)
- Setraline (Zoloft)

- Venlafaxine (Effexor)
- Imipramine (Deprenil)
- Trazadone (Desyrel)
- Desipramine (Norpramine)
- Nortriptyline (Pamelor)
- Doxepin (Sinequan)
- Clomipramine (Anafranil)
- Reboxetine (Norebox)
- Mirtazapine (Remeron)

Some Additional Do's and Don'ts

- Do be aware of sexual side effects. Tell your physician as soon as you notice a problem.
- Do not use pressure on yourself or on your partner to make sex happen; it is sure to backfire.
- Do be more sensual in the way you experience life. Tune in to the sights, sounds, and scents that are all around you. Nature walks can be a wonderful way to relax and connect to your sexual energy.

BIPOLAR DISORDER

Bipolar disorder (or what was once called "manic depression") affects 5.7 million Americans, or 2.6 percent of the population, according to the NIMH. The average age of onset is 26.5 years and the number of men and women who are diagnosed is roughly equal. Bipolar disorder is characterized by mood swings that can go from relatively mild to severe, from hypomania or mania to major depression. In bipolar I disorder, the person has had at least one episode of full mania and of major depression; in bipolar II disorder, the person has had at least one episode of hypomania and of major depression.

Before experiencing mania or hypomania, the person may be euthymic or have an overall positive mood. However, the mood continues to elevate into euphoria, or extreme happiness that does not have a strong connection to reality.

The person who is euphoric and hypomanic may feel highly energetic, optimistic, expansive, goal-directed, and creative. They may feel that they are at their best, but others around them might find them to be exhausting to be around or find their ideas to be grandiose or bigger than life. Another symptom of hypomania is feeling hypersexual; that is, they will have a high interest in sex and may act out sexually. In fact, sometimes a person is diagnosed with either form of bipolar disorder after the discovery or admission of an affair or other infidelity.

Kris and Bill

Kris worked as a designer for a prestigious fashion design company. Known for her boundless creativity, Kris would stay up around the clock when the time grew near for spring and fall fashion shows. She attended every event and every party, always networking and always aware that the next big promotion could be just around the corner. Bill often complained that they never stayed home, but he tagged along with Kris to keep her in check. In his eyes, Kris was a sexual flirt. Even with all of the energy she expended nearly 24/7, after a night out, Kris would want to come home and make love, sometimes several times in an evening.

Bill would warn Kris that she needed to slow down; he had seen what happened to her so many times after a major push. Sure enough, when the shows were over and the parties had stopped, Kris became depressed. She stayed in bed until late in the day, ignored her texts and e-mails, and cried over a feeling of failure. Worried, Bill admitted to a friend the destructive pattern he noticed in Kris. His friend shook his head in recognition; was Kris bipolar?

A person who goes from euphoria to mania will have the symptoms of hypomania, but the symptoms will be more severe and will continue for a week or more. The person will display pressured, rapid speech; racing thoughts; and an obvious decrease in their need for sleep.

Their behavior will become even more goal-directed, and in satisfying those goals, they may spend large quantities of money. They may become irritable and argumentative in a way that is out of character for them. Their grandiosity can become so exaggerated that it seems delusional; for example, they may feel that they have been selected for a special mission.

In terms of sexuality, they can become hypersexual to the point of becoming involved in risky or dangerous sexual behavior, such as seeking out the services of escorts and not practicing safe sex. Because they can also be very irritable and angry, they may feel justified in pursuing outside sexual relationships, blaming their partner for not providing enough sex. They can be highly impulsive and mix dangerous sex with alcohol or dangerous drugs (i.e., cocaine or ecstasy). Their impulsivity also puts them at risk for a suicide attempt or completion.

Peter and Mary

Peter and Mary had been together since they were both 23. Mary knew Peter as being highly charming, funny, and charismatic. Yes, he had incredible flights of fancy, like imagining himself creating a lion compound or building the repair business he operated in their garage into a multimillion-dollar enterprise by age 30, but Mary just took it in stride. For now, they were living together; she figured that once she and Peter settled down into marriage, he would stop spinning fairy tales and become more realistic.

But Peter's behavior became more erratic and difficult to explain away. He rarely slept more than three or four hours but claimed to feel refreshed and full of energy. He talked a mile a minute and his ideas about his humble repair business grew more and more unbelievable.

The worst was his sex drive. Mary, who considered herself to have a high drive, found Peter's demands insatiable because he wanted to have sex three or four times a day when she was home. Soon Mary began to work longer hours, hoping to avoid pressure from Peter. But one day she came home early with a headache, only to find Peter in bed with not one but two women—paid escorts, according to Peter.

Mary was shocked to learn that this was not the first time Peter had paid escorts for sex. In fact, after she threw him out of the house that night, she looked on his computer and at his credit card bills to discover that he had spent hundreds of dollars and seen dozens of women over the past three months. Fortunately, Peter agreed to see a psychiatrist and get medication to stabilize his mood. Mary took a wait-and-see approach to seeing how Peter managed his disorder.

In between episodes of hypomania or mania, the person may experience a normal mood (or what they describe as normal) or may become depressed, often meeting the symptoms of major depression. If the mood swings happen frequently, within days—or even hours—of each other, then bipolar disorder with rapid cycling may be diagnosed. A so-called "mixed episode" is diagnosed when the person experiences a euphoric and depressed mood all at once.

Bipolar disorder, especially mania, is managed with medication such as lithium or other mood stabilizers. Sometimes the person who is hypomanic or manic will refuse medication because they feel good, even when their behavior is obviously "off" to those around them. It is not until they experience deep depression—or even a suicide attempt—that they will admit there is a problem.

People with bipolar disorder often have difficulty staying on their medication. After they have been on medication a few weeks or a few months, they may feel that they are "cured" and lower their dosage or stop it altogether. The medications may also make them feel "flat" and make life seem purposeless, which can also cause the person to tinker with or stop their dosage. Medicating bipolar disorder can be difficult even for an experienced psychiatrist. There are many known side effects of mood stabilizers, such as tremors, weight gain, gastrointestinal distress, and mental dullness. Frequent changes in medication are common, and for many people this alone is discouraging.

Living with someone with bipolar disorder can be very challenging. Their high mood and energy can undermine their regular household routine. Hospitalizations; frequent trips to the psychiatrist; and brushes with the law; work problems; and irritability with loved ones also interfere with a positive and lasting loving relationship. In fact, there is an extremely high rate of divorce when one partner has bipolar disorder; one article in a popular magazine claimed it was as high as 90 percent. The irony is that bipolar disorder may cause a strong interest in sex, but many of the other symptoms of the disorder often make the person sexually unattractive.

Hypersexuality alone is not enough to diagnose hypomania or mania. First, hypersexuality is often subjective. If one partner wants sex daily, and the other only once a week, is the person who wants more frequent sex a "sex maniac" or "sex addict"? After all, there are couples for which daily sex is a reality. A big change in drive, along with other symptoms such as sleeplessness, loss of appetite, poor social judgment, and euphoria, can lead to a possible diagnosis of bipolar disorder.

That being said, hypersexual and goal-directed behavior that results in betrayal of a marital or relationship bond can be very tough for a couple to deal with. It can be difficult for the nonbipolar partner to separate feelings of anger from any compassion for the symptoms of bipolar disorder. Obviously, such breaches can be a contributing factor to the high rate of divorce among these couples.

* * *

Sexual Solutions When the Problem Is Bipolar Disorder

Management of the Disorder

First and foremost, the person with bipolar disorder has to take responsibility for managing his or her own illness as much as possible. If they are married or in a committed relationship, it may be helpful for the well partner to go to the initial appointments so that they can learn about bipolar disorder and the medications. Because the person with bipolar disorder may not recognize signs that demonstrate their medication is not working, it is often the partner who sees changes that may warrant a trip to the psychiatrist.

In that regard, the well partner may resent the caregiver role, whereas the person with bipolar disorder may not want to be watched. Couples would do well to regularly sit down alone or together to log any shifts in mood. They can then compare perceptions and seek outside help if they have trouble coming to an agreement or if they agree that there are obvious changes. Couples' therapy may also be helpful for handling any problems that come up because of depressive, hypomanic, or manic symptoms.

Sexual Side Effects of Mood Stabilizers

Medications that treat bipolar disorder include antidepressants and mood stabilizers, both of which can have sexual side effects. Sexual and other side effects such as weight gain, tremors, and mental dullness can lead to medication noncompliance, so it is very important that these be addressed with the physician who prescribed the medication. Unlike major depression, which may resolve within weeks or months, bipolar disorder is generally a chronic condition, and medications are usually used throughout the person's life to manage symptoms.

As we saw in the section on antidepressants, medications can have sexual side effects. However, although many people manage mild depression and dysthymia without medication and people with major depression may someday be able to wean themselves off antidepressants, people who have bipolar disorder must often be on medications for life. Not only do they have to be on medications, they must expect adjustments to medication as their bodies change with other illnesses or age. For example, a bipolar woman may find that as she enters menopause, she may be more at risk for deepening depression.

Because drug holidays are not an option and lowering one's dose may not work, the person with bipolar disorder is limited to trying medications that cause fewer sexual side effects. If you are taking an antidepressant as your mood stabilizer, then switching to one less likely to cause sexual side effects (bupropion [Wellbutrin], nefazodone [Serzone], mirtazapine [Remeron] or citalopram [Celexa]) may be a solution.

Also, newer antipsychotic medications like Respirdol and Abilify appear to cause fewer sexual side effects. However, careful monitoring and compliance need to be followed when switching medications and/or dosage to prevent a relapse of a depressive or manic episode.

Because someone needs to have been diagnosed with either hypomania or mania and major depression, you are urged to read the preceding pages on depression and sexuality, including the section on sexuality solutions. What follows are suggestions specific to the management of bipolar disorder.

Reconnecting: Coping with Relationship Betrayal

Whether the person with bipolar disorder had one affair or many, visited escorts, or engaged in looking at Internet pornography, the discovery of such activities can be painful for both parties. The person with bipolar disorder may be embarrassed or ashamed of their behavior, whereas the partner is left confused, sometimes struggling in a tug-of-war between compassion and anger.

Building trust in the wake of any relationship betrayal takes time, whether or not the cause is a psychiatric illness. Some couples are able to talk through the meaning of the sexual behavior in light of the diagnosis, particularly if the injuring partner shows remorse, insight into their condition, and is willing to take prescribed medications and work with a psychotherapist to learn how to manage their illness. However, others find that the issues are too intertwined to make sense of them, in which case a couples' therapist can help them to untangle things.

Unless the person with bipolar disorder has become psychotic, they should be considered capable of making judgments about infidelity and other unacceptable sexual behavior (e.g., compulsively using telephone sex for release). They should have a clear understanding of the consequences of future breaches of unacceptable sexual behaviors.

Negotiating Differing Sex Drives with Hypomania

If a person is hypomanic and does not suffer from depression, they often will choose not to medicate themselves. Hypomania may be annoying or draining to others, but often the person who is hypomanic enjoys feeling energetic, creative, and for some, sexually charged. However, whether a person is hypomanic or not, couples frequently differ in terms of drive as well as sexual tastes, which need to be negotiated.

Although many people would like their sex lives to be spontaneous, planning is often the key to ensuring that both partners are getting their needs met. Planning eliminates questions and worry about when the next sexual encounter is going to take place, which removes pressure. The lower-desire partner needs to understand the higher-desire partner's needs for sex, whereas the higher-desire partner needs to respect the lower-desire partner's boundaries. To ignore this is to almost guarantee a power struggle; planning is a better alternative.

How to plan? Sometimes couples go as far as to look at their calendars to see when they will both be free for the coming week. Others do not like that much structure, so having a loose guideline, such as Sunday mornings and Thursday nights, can be helpful. Planning can also occur on the fly, so that if one person feels like sex during the day or evening, they can let their partner know so that appropriate arrangements can be made to take care of the housework, kids, etc., before the main event.

Negotiating Sexual Tastes

Sometimes hypersexuality is associated with unconventional sexual behavior. The person with bipolar disorder who is hypersexual may want to explore types of sexual activities that some partners may consider to be outside of the norm (e.g., anal sex for heterosexual couples or the use of light bondage as part of foreplay).

It is not beyond imagination to see that the bipolar person who is hypersexual and becomes sexually frustrated may also become irritable. Fearful that the partner who is bipolar may look for gratification outside of the committed relationship, sometimes people will give into their partner's tastes. Although occasionally doing so may not cause much harm, a sexual relationship that includes coercion is far from ideal.

Sexual exploration can be pleasurable for both partners if some general guidelines are followed. First and foremost, there must be good communication. Partners must be able to communicate their needs and their limits and to listen to one another without judgment. Neither partner should belittle the other for either wanting to be adventurous or staying within the lines.

If the hypersexual partner has unconventional needs, it can be helpful for partners to learn to negotiate with one another. For example, if the hypersexual partner enjoys pornography and the other does not, but does like to read erotic stories, then the couple can switch off or they can agree that these activities can be conducted individually, in private.

However, the most important ingredient is that the couple stays emotionally connected during sex. The person who is hypersexual needs to demonstrate that they are not so much using their partner to fulfill a need, but that they are capable of expressing warm feelings during their encounter. When the nonbipolar partner is uninterested in experimentation, they can say so in a loving, nonjudgmental way.

RESOURCES

Books

Addis, Michael E., and Christopher R. Martell. *Overcoming Depression One Step at a Time: The New Behavioral Activation Approach to Getting Your Life Back*. Oakland, CA: New Harbinger Publications, 2004.

Basco, Monica Ramirez. *The Bipolar Workbook: Tools for Controlling Your Mood Swings*. New York: The Guilford Press, 2005.

Fast, Julie A., and John D. Preston. *Loving Someone with Bipolar Disorder*. Oakland, CA: New Harbinger Publications, 2004.

Williams, Mark, John D. Teasdale, Zindel V. Segal, and Jon Kabat-Zinn. *The Mindful Way through Depression: Freeing Yourself from Chronic Unhappiness*. New York: The Guilford Press, 2007.

Online Resources

National Institute of Mental Health. Bipolar Disorder: http://www.nimh.nih.gov/health/publications/bipolar-disorder/complete-index.shtml.

National Institute of Mental Health. Depression: http://www.nimh.nih.gov/health/publications/depression/complete-index.shtml.

Chapter Four

ANXIETY DISORDERS

GENERALIZED ANXIETY AND OBSESSIVE-COMPULSIVE DISORDER

Approximately 40 million Americans, or about around 18 percent of adults, have an anxiety disorder that causes mental worry and physical tension. However, almost everyone knows what it means to feel anxious. For example, most people understand that meeting a new group of people might cause someone to feel nervous. The symptoms of anxiety must last at least six months and interfere with a person's ability to function at work, home, or in relationships for a diagnosis of an anxiety disorder to be made. Also, anxiety disorders frequently are diagnosed with other mental or physical illnesses, such as depression, pain and somatic disorders, and even autism. Sometimes people who are diagnosed with alcohol or substance abuse or dependence have an underlying anxiety problem they are trying to mask.

There are several different types of anxiety disorders, with generalized anxiety disorder (GAD), social phobia, obsessive-compulsive disorder (OCD), and post-traumatic stress disorder (PTSD) being most commonly diagnosed. These disorders can cause various sexual problems in general, including:

- Erectile dysfunction
- Premature or rapid ejaculation
- Delayed or inhibited ejaculation in men
- Problems with sexual arousal
- Anorgasmia (lack of orgasm) in women
- Performance anxiety
- Avoidance of sex and low sex drive

Each disorder has different, although, somewhat overlapping, symptoms, such as pessimism, negative thinking, overgrown fears, muscle tension, fatigue, and so forth. Because they are so common and because of the stigma of having a mental disorder, many people live with these problems, only becoming concerned when they themselves no longer enjoy sex or a partner becomes discouraged about their sexual relationship. Without dealing with the underlying anxiety disorder, it can be difficult to treat the sexual symptoms.

GAD and Social Phobia

GAD, the most common anxiety disorder, is marked by excessive worry, difficulty relaxing or concentrating, fear of losing control, fear of rejection by others, and feelings of dread. From a physical standpoint, a person with GAD may experience muscle aches, fatigue, stomach upset, jitteriness, or difficulty falling and staying asleep. All of these symptoms make it difficult for someone to feel sexual interest or arousal. Sometimes symptoms of anxiety themselves can cause such discomfort that sexual performance, arousal, and desire are all negatively affected. Sweating, blushing, shaking, and feeling jittery all have the potential to get in the way of pleasure.

In turn, symptoms can be triggered in people raised in a sexually restrictive home or community. Although it is natural to be nervous with a new partner, ongoing fears about sexual performance can cause serious emotional and relationship damage. People with GAD or social phobia are frequently unaware of its effect on their ability to enjoy life and experience pleasure. A curious study of heterosexual women with an anxiety disorder suggested that they might, in fact, be physically aroused as measured by such changes in the vagina as increased lubrication, yet be mentally unaware that they are sexually excited.

> **Connie and Bill**
> Connie and Bill have very little sex in their marriage of three years. Although Connie found sex exciting at first, she soon found herself feeling overwhelmed by working and taking care of their household. Laundry, dishes, housekeeping, yard work, grocery shopping, and cooking—there was so much to do that sometimes Connie even set her alarm to get up in the middle of the night to move clothing from the washing machine to the dryer. She just could not understand how Bill could find the energy to want sex, let alone have it.

Many women and, although less frequently, men find it difficult to relax when it comes to responsibilities. Instead of thinking erotic thoughts when bedtime comes around, they are mired in a list of "to do's." However, it is also possible that anxiety about chores is a distraction from anxiety about sex. When couples first engage in sexual activity, chemicals in the brain called neurotransmitters (e.g., dopamine) make sex very exciting. Later, when a partner is more aware of being frankly naked and sexual, they may become inhibited. Rather than dealing with the sexual fears head on, they may develop an aversion to sex but blame it on how busy and tired they are.

The biggest fear of someone with social phobia, also known as performance anxiety, is that they will be harshly judged and rejected by others. Physically, the person with performance anxiety may blush, stammer, feel shaky or clammy, have an upset stomach, nausea, muscle tension, or twitching. Psychologically, they may build up worry for days before a big event (e.g., lovemaking on an anniversary, perhaps) in what is sometimes called "anticipatory anxiety." They feel self-conscious, watching every move and thought, which is definitely a downer when it comes to the bedroom.

Because sex requires a certain level of openness and vulnerability, knowing one's partner is of little comfort when worrying about how good one is as a lover. A person who suffers from social anxiety often becomes so absorbed in making sure that their partner is sexually satisfied that they will forget their own pleasure. Consequently, they may have difficulty becoming or staying sexually aroused. This, in turn, can lead to difficulty with orgasm and subsequent loss of interest in sex. As each of the following scenarios demonstrate, anxiety can affect people in different ways.

Lewis

Shy as a child, Lewis continued to struggle with social embarrassment into adulthood. Although he was able to cope well enough to hold down a responsible job, dating was very difficult. However, when he finally met a woman he felt comfortable with, the most embarrassing thing he could imagine happened: Not even having undressed, he ejaculated while he and his partner were exploring one another's bodies. Although he desperately wanted to connect with a woman, Lewis was too humiliated to even consider dating for a few years after that incident, let alone have sex.

Naomi

Every time Naomi knew she had to get up in front of a group to give a talk, she spent the night before holding her stomach, doubled over in cramps. However, she never connected her performance anxiety in the classroom and workplace with the fears she had in the bedroom. Naomi worried about whether she could help her partner have a good orgasm, if she was a good kisser, if she smelled clean, how her breasts looked, whether her partner noticed the dry patch of skin on her shin, and on and on.

Publicly, she made a big show of liking sex, but privately she thought of it as pointless. Pretty soon the only time she could have an orgasm when she was alone with a vibrator and concentrated very hard. After awhile, she could not have orgasm at all and lost interest in sex altogether, eventually driving away a person who might otherwise have been a good partner.

Graham

Graham considered himself a great partner in bed. He enjoyed a lusty sex life with his wife; sex was the way he relaxed. However, coming up on 45, he noticed that his erections were not as hard as they once were. Graham tried not to think about it, but then one night that was filled with wining, dining, and dancing, Graham could not even get an erection. Graham was certain that his sex life was over. Ever since that evening, Graham lost his erection every time he was about to enter his wife for intercourse. Soon, his worried thoughts filled his day and he had trouble sleeping at night.

Eventually, Graham called a urologist, who prescribed one of the medications that seemed guaranteed to give a man an erection. Although Graham was skeptical, he took his pill and waited. No erection. Then he remembered that the pill did not give him an erection—he needed to be engaged in sex. So he told his wife that he had taken a pill and asked her to make love. The plan backfired, with his wife crying about the fact that Graham no longer found her sexy enough to make love without medication. Although nothing could be further from the truth, Graham was now more confused than ever.

Like many men, Graham's erectile dysfunction (ED) was not initially caused by anxiety alone. Although he pressured himself a bit about having an especially good lovemaking session, most likely his ED was caused by food, wine, and fatigue. However, because Graham bought into the myth that a "real" man should be able to perform sexually any time, anywhere, and under any circumstance, the fact that he "failed" played into deep-rooted fears about his masculinity.

* * *

Sexual Solutions When the Problem Is Generalized Anxiety

Research has repeatedly shown that the best solution for mild to moderate anxiety disorders is cognitive behavioral therapy (CBT). CBT addresses all three symptom areas: thoughts, physical symptoms, and behaviors. For moderate to severe anxiety, antidepressant medication such as Paxil or Lexapro is added as part of long-term treatment. For short-term treatment, a fast-acting medication such as Xanax might be prescribed to help someone be able to get through a very stressful period. Because such medications are physically and psychologically addictive, care must be taken to use as directed.

The benefit of adding medication is that a person can learn the tools of managing anxiety while on medication for 6–12 months and then try managing on their own without drugs. However, the problem with antidepressant medication is that people have a risk of experiencing sexual side effects. Also, many people stay on the medication for long periods of time, avoiding self-help or psychotherapy. The decision of whether or not to use medication should be discussed with a psychiatrist who is well trained in understanding how to treat anxiety disorders.

Whether a person who has GAD or social anxiety is treated for anxiety in general or for anxiety that affects sexuality in particular will often depend on the presenting problem. If a person sees a psychiatrist or psychotherapist to overcome an intense fear of public speaking, then the focus likely will be on that problem. However, because of shame and embarrassment, not only do patients not tell the practitioner about the sexual anxiety, the practitioner may not ask. Therefore, even people who seek help for anxiety may not make the connection between their psychological state and their sex life.

Anxiety affects a couple's relationship in several ways. Anxiety has a way of being "contagious," so that one partner senses when the other is tense and then also has difficulty letting go and enjoying sex. In this way, one partner's sexual anxiety can become a burden to the nonanxious partner. Also, it can be easy for the nonanxious partner to dismiss or minimize the anxious partner's thoughts and feelings. However, anxiety is real and can be difficult to understand or manage without the proper tools. Therefore, what follows are approaches to managing anxiety when it particularly affects sex.

Deep Breathing

Although it may sound simple, deep breathing has many benefits, including muscle relaxation and a positive distraction from worry. It can be the foundational step of managing almost any type of anxiety in almost any situation. Using one's own breath to achieve calm is self-empowering and can be done discreetly.

Deep breathing during sex may require patience and support on the part of the partner. When the anxious person becomes nervous, they can quietly breathe while giving or receiving pleasure, or they can ask to take a brief break, during which they can stay physically connected (e.g., by spooning, cuddling, or holding hands). Once they have managed their anxiety, sexual activity can resume.

The best way to learn about the benefits of deep breathing is to practice frequently throughout the day. Begin by finding a regular activity that you do during which you can practice deep breathing, for example, waiting at a red light or while waiting for a program to boot up on your computer. By learning to relax throughout the day, you will reset your baseline and so be less anxious about sex if and when you decide to make love.

Negative Thoughts about Sex

A partner with anxiety will have negative, pessimistic thoughts about sex. The thoughts may or may not be expressed. In fact, thoughts may be so automatic that they go unnoticed but still have an effect. Becoming more aware of one's own thoughts can be helpful, and in some relationships, the nonanxious partner can gently point out when they occur. Once one is aware of the specific thoughts they are having, they can find ways to counter them, replacing negative thoughts with more realistic, positive thoughts.

- *Black-and-white thinking.* Example: I have to give my partner a fantastic orgasm or I will be rejected. Counter: My partner and I can enjoy sex for lots of different reasons.
- *Mind reading.* Example: My partner thinks that I look silly while lying naked on the bed. Counter: I don't really know what my partner is thinking. During sex, I'll focus on how I feel instead of how I look.
- *Catastrophizing.* Example: If I don't have an erection, it will be the end of my marriage. Counter: My partner and I can work through this together. We can try other things to have pleasure together.
- *Minimizing.* Example: My partner's complaints about my inhibitions are no big deal. Counter: I need to take my partner's complaints seriously and understand that I can become less inhibited.
- *"Should" statements.* Example: I should be more turned on right now than I am. Counter: Who is to say how turned on I should be? It's okay to feel what I feel at any given moment.
- *Discounting the positive.* Example: Just because I had an orgasm this time doesn't mean it will happen again. Counter: I enjoy sex with and without orgasm, although the experiences may be different.

What is wonderful about learning these countering techniques is that if you can learn to use them with sexual behaviors, you can learn to use them in other areas of your life. Sometimes, too, when one partner is anxious and begins to feel down, it can rub off on the other partner. By (gently) monitoring each other, you can both learn to feel better and more optimistic about sex.

Mindfulness

Mindfulness is an ancient idea that is gaining more and more mainstream attention. Mindfulness is often suggested to people who have anxiety and depression because it takes the focus off of worry about the past or future and places it on living calmly and certainly in the present moment. One researcher also found that mindfulness can be helpful for women who find it difficult to become aroused during sex. It is a tool that is useful in daily life, but it can also help an anxious partner lose himself in the act of lovemaking.

Mindfulness is not achieved in an "aha!" moment, nor is it a constant state. Mindfulness is called a practice because it has to be learned and experienced over and over again if it is to have benefit. In fact, you may find being mindful difficult at first because it is very counter to our Western way of frequently being busy and stressed.

So what then does it mean to be mindful? It can be taught in many ways, but what I have found helpful is to ask people to focus on their senses. Your senses—your sight, hearing, smell, taste, and touch—are all cued to letting you know what is happening in the present moment. They keep you focused on reality, rather than on the chatter in your mind. I also like to use the analogy of driving or riding in a car: You cannot be where you were, and you cannot be where you are going. You can only be where you are, at any moment. So stop worrying about the past and the future, and focus on what is happening now. Detach from your thoughts and live.

It can be easier to initially try mindfulness in daily life rather than in the bedroom, especially if that is where you feel the most anxious. Try taking a walk some place in nature. Calm your thoughts. If you find yourself thinking, then gently tell your mind to quiet itself or imagine your thoughts floating through you like a breeze going through window curtains. Focus on your surroundings and the pleasure they bring to you. Notice how, as you become absorbed in paying attention, you become less distracted by your thoughts.

In the bedroom, you can also put your focus on what is happening in the moment. When your mind drifts away from lovemaking and the pleasure that you are experiencing, bring it gently back to what is happening. If you are the active partner, stay with your actions rather than your thoughts. If you are the passive partner, pay attention to sensation. The best sex often happens when you are absorbed in what you are doing and let the world fall away.

You can learn more about mindfulness in Appendix 2.

THE BENEFITS OF SEX

Countering negative thoughts about sex is one path to being more comfortable, but another is looking directly at the reasons that sex is pleasurable. These include:

Physical benefits
- Cardiovascular circulation
- Muscle relaxation
- Improved sleep
- Hormone balance
- Enhanced pelvic floor function

Emotional benefits
- Feeling connected to a partner
- Nonverbal expression of feelings
- Experience of joy or contentment
- Improved mood
- Feeling complete as a gendered person

OCD

OCD is a serious mental illness that is sometimes confused with obsessive-compulsive personality disorder (OCPD). Although the two disorders have some overlapping symptoms, symptoms of OCD are generally more difficult to control or to change. (For a discussion of OCPD and sexuality, please see pages 94–95.) OCD is marked by obsessions, or unwanted thoughts or images that are upsetting, involuntary, and repetitive. Obsessions are followed by compulsions, which are actions that the person takes to temporarily relieve the anxiety caused by the obsessions. For example, a person may have an obsession that their home could burn down. Therefore, they check all of the appliances and pilot lights before they leave their house.

Some types of obsessions are more common than others. Typical obsessions include cleanliness, orderliness, concerns about germs and illness, fear of disaster, and religious questions or ideas. Compulsions include repetitive counting, washing, checking, and taking great pains to avoid coming into contact with a feared substance or situation (e.g., driving many extra miles to avoid getting into traffic because of fear of a terrible traffic collision).

The effect of OCD on romance and quality of life has been well documented. People involved with someone with OCD find that they must adhere to or support rules that may make no real or logical sense. They may resent the time, energy, and sometimes money that are put into their partner's compulsive activities. They may even come to feel as if they, too, have OCD. Conversely, marital and relationship distress can sometimes exacerbate an individual's OCD symptoms.

There is not much research on this topic, but one study does suggest that women with OCD are more likely than women without OCD to have trouble experiencing vaginal lubrication and orgasm. They may also experience sexual activity as being disgusting. Interestingly, the women in the study with OCD had sexual intercourse as frequently as women in the control group. The authors suggested that this is because the women with OCD understood the benefits of sex for their intimate relationship, even if they did not much enjoy it.

Carol and Tony

Carol worried so much about dental health that she avoided eating hard foods and spent nearly an hour every morning and evening brushing and flossing her teeth. She saw a dental hygienist every month and visited her dentist often. Nothing her husband Tony could say or do could dissuade her from her belief that her teeth were going to break or fall out if she did not put excessive energy into their care. Carol never noticed that her sex drive had completely disappeared, but Tony did. Carol's response was to spend even more time on her teeth at night, hoping that Tony would fall asleep and forget about having sex.

OCD with Sexual Content

Sexual obsessions and compulsions are also common, affecting approximately 25 percent of those diagnosed with OCD. Obsessions can be about many things, including worries about whether one is homosexual, fears about AIDS and other sexually transmitted diseases, being unfaithful, or concerns about fertility or pregnancy. For example, a woman who loses interest in a man she once thought she loved might develop a concern that she has become a lesbian. She looks at each woman she sees, trying to determine if she is attracted to someone of the same sex. Or a man might be very careful to wash his hands for several minutes after touching his genitals, fearing that he could impregnate a woman if he touched her. Because there is very little research on this type of OCD, people who have sexual-type OCD are sometimes misdiagnosed as having an unconscious sexual wish, a sexual identity crisis, or a paraphilia (deviant sexual behavior). Research suggests that people whose OCD focuses on bodily secretions have the most difficulty with having sex with a partner, which appears to be related to common fears about contamination. Although such obsessions may not interfere with sexual function, they do appear to affect sexual satisfaction. The secretions themselves, and any associated odors, can cause disgust and create avoidance.

Sexual obsessions are not the same as sexual fantasies. Sexual fantasies are generally pleasant and benign; they do not cause undue shame or guilt. Sexual fantasies are often what drive sexual desire. A sexual obsession is an unwelcome thought that the person with OCD would not want to act out. They also usually do not cause sexual arousal. The obsessions are unpleasant, and the person wants them to stop.

Lydia and Frank
"Remember not to kiss my mouth!"
    "Use this antibacterial hand wash before you touch my vagina."
    "I don't care if you shower, I can't stand the smell of oral sex."
    Frank found that Lydia's fears and disgust about germs and odors took all of the joy and spontaneity out of having sex. Although he voiced his complaints, Lydia turned a deaf ear. She just had an indescribable feeling that if she was not careful about dirt during sex, she could become somehow contaminated or polluted. When she and Frank did have sex, there was no afterplay because Lydia would jump up and take an immediate shower. Although she had been warned not to do so, she also used an old-fashioned vinegar douche to clean away any semen or vaginal secretions. Truth be known, if it were up to Lydia, she and Frank would never have sex at all.

Tom and Kelly
Married for nine years, Kelly was becoming exceedingly tired of sex with Tom. Tom needed to have sex in the same way, in the same exact position, thinking the same

exact fantasy every time they were intimate. If something disrupted him—a dog barking outside or a squeak in the mattress—Tom would have to stop, take a deep breath, rearrange himself, and go back to having intercourse and running his fantasy through again from the top. Sometimes they would end up having intercourse for almost 45 minutes, with Kelly being as patient as possible. Although sex was not the most important part of marriage for Kelly, she found herself growing more and more irritable with Tom and his ritualized approach to sex, so much so that she was considering divorce.

Although people sometimes do not recognize that their thoughts are false, even those who do have that recognition will say that their irrational thought feels real. They will still have a very difficult time stopping their unwanted thoughts altogether, although they may temporarily stop when faced with a logical argument or reassurance from others.

* * *

Sexual Solutions When the Problem Is OCD

Treatment

Perhaps the most important solution for OCD that gets in the way of sexual pleasure is to get therapeutic treatment. Although it can feel embarrassing or shameful to admit that one has a problem, the alternative—letting the problem fester until it spoils a relationship—is a poor one. The current treatment for OCD is CBT. Medication such as Prozac (fluoxetene) can also be beneficial, either at the beginning of treatment for mild to moderate OCD, or for their long-term benefit for moderate to severe forms. Unfortunately, approximately one-third of people who take such medications may have sexual side effects such as low desire, delayed ejaculation, or ED.

Treatment is often difficult, and there will be setbacks. If the relationship is to survive, the non-OCD spouse needs to learn as much as possible about the illness. For example, it does not help to explain to the person with OCD over and over again that one of their beliefs is irrational. The person with OCD generally knows this but will think and act as usual because it feels as if it must be done this way. The non-OCD person also needs to understand that they do not have to participate in the rituals such as checking the entire house to make sure all the windows are locked. Separating the person from their illness is also helpful, because then partners can identify symptoms, figure out whose problem they are, and how to work on them.

When the problem is sexual obsession, the psychotherapeutic treatment is generally what is called exposure-response prevention (ERP). Basically, the afflicted person is exposed to their obsession many, many times while they cope with their anxiety until they no longer feel very upset about their thinking.

Acceptance

In some cases, the best course of action is acceptance of mild OCD symptoms, although they may interfere somewhat with a feeling of intimacy. In Lydia and Frank's case, for example Frank can accept that Lydia does not like the feeling of his saliva on her mouth. Because she enjoys most other forms of sex play and is an active partner, he can focus on what he can enjoy with Lydia instead of limitations. In fact, focusing on limitations may make someone even more upset and anxious so that the behaviors that the obsessive person will permit become more and more narrow in range.

Taking a relaxed approach that keeps in mind the larger picture—that having a satisfying sex life with a caring partner is more important than a deep kiss—can also help couples come to terms. Also, if the obsessive-compulsive behavior is understood as such, it can be much easier to see it for what it is—a symptom of an anxiety disorder—instead of as withholding affection.

Letting Go and Enjoying Pleasure

Most people understand the idea that to have orgasm, one has to be able to stop thinking, concentrate on sensation, and let go. For the partner with OCD, especially the female partner, this can be a difficult task. Mindfulness, which is described in Appendix 2, can be helpful in this regard. By focusing on sensory experiences instead of thoughts, a partner can more easily stay in the present moment.

PTSD

It is normal for a person who has been exposed to frightening or catastrophic events to feel anxious in their aftermath. However, sometimes the effects of a traumatic event can linger for weeks and months after it has occurred. In fact, for a person diagnosed with PTSD, symptoms such as flashbacks, bad dreams, feelings of guilt and depression, avoidance of certain people or situations, and negative emotions like rage can sometimes be triggered years after the event, although the person may have seemed fine.

When it comes to PTSD and sexual problems, the most likely traumatic cause is sexual abuse or violence. It makes sense that a person who was frightened, exploited, or felt powerless in regard to sexual activity would feel terribly upset. But other catastrophes such as being in or seeing combat, a traffic accident, or a natural disaster can also get in the way of a person's ability to function sexually.

PTSD and Childhood Sexual Abuse

Approximately one in four women and one in six men are thought to have experienced childhood sexual abuse (CSA). No one really knows the true numbers because these statistics are based on actual reports, and because of its embarrassing and stigmatizing nature, many episodes of CSA go unreported. Also, not everyone who experiences CSA will have sexual problems. But those who do may experience symptoms including low desire, difficulty becoming aroused, struggling with orgasm or ejaculation, ED, sexual aversion or disgust, or a history of sexual impulsivity or acting out.

In addition to sexual problems, psychological problems can get in the way of a CSA survivor's ability to be intimate on all sorts of levels. Most CSA occurs between a child or teen and someone they know, so the sense of betrayal can be very deep. In turn, that betrayal leads to a lack of trust and feeling of safety in future relationships. Also, many CSA survivors emotionally numb themselves so that they can cope with bad feelings like shame and disgust. If the trauma was severe enough (e.g., in the case of incest), the numbing may go so far as to cause the person to dissociate, or disconnect from reality.

Suspicion, fear, numbing, and dissociation are all understandable in the face of a real threat, but in the person with PTSD, they generalize to everyone, even a loving partner who cares for them. In fact, these negative emotions may not even be apparent to that partner until the relationship becomes more physically and emotionally intimate, when the close connection begins to feel more like a threat than a comfort. At that point, the partner may find himself or herself in a relationship with someone who is withdrawn, moody, having panic attacks and flashbacks, and disgusted by the idea of sexual contact. Especially when the couple is physically intimate, the survivor may have confusion between the past and present reality, flashbacks, and body memories that are linked to feelings of vulnerability and helplessness. The survivor may also feel betrayed when his or her partner has enjoyed sex.

All of this emotional volatility can lead to the partner of the survivor experiencing some degree of vicarious trauma. The partner may become confused, distressed, and even depressed because what had seemed like a loving sexual relationship dissolves into misunderstanding and blame. The partner may feel as if they are walking in a minefield, uncertain if something they will say or do will trigger a memory and ignite an enormous emotional response. Unfortunately, this can cause even an empathic partner to become defensive and angry in return, unwittingly putting himself or herself in the role of an abuser. In fact, in the survivor's need for control, paired with the partner's confusion, hurt, and anger, couples can sometimes seesaw back and forth between the roles of savior. The male partner of a survivor may develop ED or premature ejaculation, low sexual desire, or sexual aversion out of fear of emotional or physical pain.

Memories in the form of flashbacks or sensations can remain hidden from consciousness for many years. A so-called "trigger" may bring them back into consciousness. Triggers can range from a chance meeting with the perpetrator to a partner simply skimming a hand across a sensitive place (e.g., the upper thigh or lower abdomen) during foreplay. Odors ranging from cologne to alcohol, room lighting, the feel of sheets on one's body, or the way a sexual request is made have all been reported to me as triggers. Triggers can evoke a range of responses from the survivor, from dissociation and numbing to tears and rage.

Although men and women suffer, men are especially reluctant to tell anyone that abuse has ever occurred. Men may struggle with issues of sexual identity and masculinity, especially if the perpetrator was male.

PTSD and Combat

Estimates are that about as many as 8 percent of Gulf War and 30 percent of Vietnam War veterans have a diagnosis of PTSD. When it comes to sex, PTSD affects veterans in many ways. Some veterans may not only have seen and done terrible but necessary things, but they may also have been injured. Physical and psychological injuries can have a negative effect not only on the ability to have sex, but also on the ability to be emotionally intimate. Seeing and participating in battle can cause distrust, emotional numbing, hypervigilance (constant watching of the environment), flashbacks, and nightmares.

In various studies of male combat veterans with PTSD, about 80 percent complained of dissatisfaction with their sexual experiences. The most frequent complaint—about 69 percent of men—reported problems with erectile function, but veterans also complained about premature ejaculation. Flat mood and lack of arousal in PTSD vets may underlie sexual problems. However, there is also a high rate of medical problems, such as cardiovascular disease, and psychiatric problems, such as depression, among veterans with PTSD, which can also lead to problems with sexual function. Prescription medications such as SSRIs may also be a contributing factor.

Sexual Solutions When the Problem Is PTSD

Treatment

Psychotherapy can be of great help to the survivor of sexual abuse in helping him or her develop more accurate beliefs about the abuse itself, increasing a sense of self-esteem, the management of angry responses to triggers, ways of dealing with flashbacks, and increasing trust in others. However, the partner's own need for therapeutic support and guidance are often neglected. Psychotherapy can help educate the partner about the effects of abuse, making the survivor's reactions less personal and generating appropriate empathy. Current research suggests that trauma can create long-lasting and perhaps permanent changes in the brain and nervous system, making the feelings and behaviors associated with survival less under conscious control than one might believe. At some point in the survivor's treatment, couples' therapy may also be indicated so that they can work through the difficulties and strain that CSA has placed on their relationship.

As potentially helpful as therapy might be, there are a few cautions. Therapy itself can trigger any number of unwanted but powerful reactions, including flashbacks, body memories, rage, and so forth. Additionally, although many patients and therapists do important work together, there can be an assumption that a romantic connection and sexual function will automatically return as the trauma is worked through. In fact, this may not occur and, unfortunately, in my own practice, I have had clients tell me that their therapist never asked about sexual dysfunction (perhaps out of embarrassment, perhaps because not every survivor has sexual problems) and that they themselves were too embarrassed to bring it up. If there are specific sexual concerns, then a sex therapist (someone trained as a psychotherapist and specializing in sexuality) may be of assistance.

Safety and Trust

Establishing safety and trust in anticipation of sexual activity is critical for the PTSD survivor. The most important ingredient is communication, in that the survivor needs to be able to identify what increases or decreases a feeling of trust. Often survivors have rigid conscious or unconscious ideas about where, when, and how sex should take place in order to ensure a measure of control. Sometimes this need for control overrides or interferes with the desire for pleasure, both for the survivor and the partner.

Being respectful of this need, a healthier way to create safety would be to discuss what the survivor needs and then find multiple ways to fulfill it. For example, the survivor might discover that he or she feels better about a partner initiating sex at certain times or in certain ways (e.g., having sex in the morning after a good night's sleep, in a place other than the couple's bed such as a shower or tub, or nonverbally with a note or a signal). Attention can also be paid to the physical environment (e.g., ensuring that there is a lock on the bedroom door, having appropriate lighting, making the bedroom cheerful and welcoming, and so forth).

Managing Confusion

One of the problems mentioned is that survivors sometimes have difficulty distinguishing between past and present, which can happen at all kinds of intimate times, including during sexual activity. If both partners are attuned to this, the partner can help the survivor stay in the present moment with reminders and assurances. For example, the partner can remind the survivor that he or she is not the perpetrator, that they have a loving connection and a healthy reason to be intimate, and that the survivor has choices about what is to happen next.

It can also be helpful if the survivor can identify the triggers that bring confusion and anger into play. The couple can then together problem-solve to make them less problematic. For example, if a survivor cannot tolerate having a hand on his or her thigh, then the couple can agree that holding hands while watching television is safe. Being able to talk things through, rather than acting out emotionally, can bring the couple closer together.

Problems with Arousal

Emotional numbing and dissociation can also interfere with the ability to enjoy sexual sensations and pleasure. The physical sensations of sexual arousal are not much different than anxiety: rapid heartbeat, quicker respiration, tingling, and so forth. Arousal may also bring with it memory triggers as well as shame for having felt pleasure, even if the touch was unwanted. Thus, the survivor may have difficulty becoming excited during lovemaking, in turn losing interest and developing an aversion altogether.

The sensate focus activities described in appendix 1 can be helpful to survivors because the progression is slow, from taking turns touching each other's extremities (hands, arms, legs, and feet), to mutual touching and intercourse. Deep breathing, described in the first part of this chapter, can help the survivor regulate any flooding of memories or bad feelings during the sensate focus activities. The activities can be modified so that couples can start with a simple hand or foot massage and work their way through more intimate touching.

Mindfulness, described in appendix 2, is another way to gain a feeling of control. By staying in the present moment and concentrating on sensual information rather than images, the survivor can quiet the mind and body. Mindfulness can help the survivor become nonjudgmental about themselves, which alleviates shame and guilt. This can also make it easier to leave the abuse where it belongs, in the survivor's past.

RESOURCES

Books

Bass, Ellen. *The Courage to Heal: A Guide for Women Survivors of Child Sexual Abuse.* New York: Harper Perennial, 1988.

Bourne, Edmund J. *The Anxiety & Phobia Workbook.* Oakland, CA: New Harbinger Publications, 1990.

Burns, David D. *When Panic Attacks: The New, Drug-Free Anxiety Therapy That Can Change Your Life.* New York: Broadway Books, 2007.

Carmin, C. *Obsessive-Compulsive Disorder Demystified: An Essential Guide for Understanding and Living with OCD.* Cambridge, MA: Da Capo Press, 2009.

Foa, E. A., and R. Wilson. *Stop Obsessing! How to Overcome Your Obsessions and Compulsions,* Revised ed. New York: Bantam, 2001.

Maltz, Wendy. *The Sexual Healing Journey: A Guide for Survivors of Sexual Abuse.* New York: Harper Perennial, 1992.

Matsakis, Aphrodite. *I Can't Get Over It: A Handbook for Trauma Survivors.* Oakland, CA: New Harbinger Publications, 1992.

Orange, Cynthia. *Shock Waves: A Practical Guide to Living with a Loved One's PTSD.* Center City, MN: Hazelden Publishing, 2010.

Online Resources

Anxiety Disorders Association of America: http://www.adaa.org.

David Baldwin's Trauma Information Pages: http://www.trauma-pages.com.

MedlinePlus. Obsessive Compulsive Disorder: http://www.nlm.nih.gov/medlineplus/obsessivecompulsivedisorder.html.

National Institute of Mental Health. Anxiety Disorders: http://www.nimh.nih.gov/health/topics/anxiety-disorders/index.shtml.

U.S. Department of Veterans Affairs National Center for PTSD: http://www.ptsd.va.gov.

Chapter Five

BODY-RELATED DISORDERS

Because this book is specifically about mental disorders and sexuality, I have taken the liberty of grouping the disorders in this chapter differently than one would find them classified in the DSM. For example, in the DSM, sexual pain disorders such as dyspareunia (a condition in which a woman experiences pain with intercourse) are grouped with sexual disorders, but pain disorders are grouped under somatoform disorders. Body dysmorphic disorder (BDD; diagnosed when a person is abnormally preoccupied with a part of their body) and hypochondriasis disorder (HD; excessive worry about having an illness or disease) are classified as somatoform disorders rather than anxiety disorders. Instead, I have grouped them based on the fact that they are all body-focused problems that can interfere with sexuality and relationships. The problems included in this chapter are:

- Pain disorders
- Sexual pain disorders
- Body dysmorphic disorder
- Hypochondriasis

PAIN DISORDERS AND SEXUALITY

In the United States, pain is the most common reason for physician visits. It is a symptom that is part of many medical conditions, and it can interfere significantly with one's quality of life. In the DSM-IV, there are two categories for pain disorder—pain associated with psychological factors and pain associated with psychological factors plus a general medical condition such as arthritis or cancer.

Pain is very complex. Many people believe that if a physician talks about psychological causes or makes a referral to a psychotherapist or psychiatrist, then the pain isn't real. But that is not the case. The pain truly exists; it is just that the exact cause, nature, and treatment might be unclear. There may be other factors (e.g., depression or anxiety) that make it harder to decrease or turn down the sensation of pain.

For example, if you drop a hammer on your bare toe, you undoubtedly will feel pain. Your toe may throb; it may even break. You will need treatment. But after awhile, you would expect your toe to stop hurting and start healing. But sometimes when a person continues to experience physical pain, there is no direct physical cause. For example, if the toe pain made someone depressed because they could not walk for several weeks, they might feel isolated and sad. The pain may continue past the point when one would expect the pain to have healed. If a physician looks for a direct physical cause, none will be found. But that does not mean that the person is "faking" the pain.

Pain that is caused by medical illnesses can become more complicated by psychological issues. If a person has fibromyalgia (chronic widespread pain), the experience of having it can lead to depression, which can in turn make healing from episodes of fibromyalgia more complicated. In addition, there can be so-called "secondary gain" from having a pain disorder.

Even relationship dynamics can affect how a person copes with pain. If a person normally asks for or receives very little needed emotional attention from their partner, a PD may give them a reason to gain sympathy, either consciously or unconsciously. A person with PD may also find pain an excuse not to participate in uninteresting activities, from grocery shopping to sex.

WHAT IS SECONDARY GAIN?

It may be difficult to understand or accept the idea that someone may derive some benefit from having a chronic physical or mental illness. After all, people in general do not ask or wish to be ill. But if you think about it, most everyone has had the experience of calling work or canceling a social engagement because of an illness and then feeling relieved.

In medicine and psychiatry, secondary gain is understood to be conscious or unconscious (within or not within the person's awareness). For example, the ill partner may consciously manipulate the well partner into doing chores that they know they are capable of doing themselves. Or the ill partner may unconsciously learn that complaining about their condition gets them much-needed or wanted attention from their partner.

Sometimes secondary gain is hard for couples themselves to see at work in their relationship. When an ill person's treatment does not go well or as expected, physicians and psychologists may suspect that there is secondary gain at work. A careful evaluation of illness behaviors and responses may be necessary to understand and correct this relationship pattern.

Pain is associated with many different types of illnesses and diseases. Pain that is acute and resolved with time, medications, or both may cause some annoyance or frustration when it comes to sex, but this is generally brief. However, chronic pain that is difficult to manage or affects the partner's ability to function can interfere with a couple's sex life. Examples of such conditions include fibromyalgia, chronic fatigue syndrome, myofascial pain disorder, arthritis, multiple sclerosis, certain types of cancer, sciatica, temporomandibular joint disorder (TMJ), and migraine headaches. The impact of these conditions on relationships and intimacy can be substantial. Both partners can experience frustration and lose patience and compassion for each other when pain seems to be an excuse for not having sex. Chronic pain can also limit what a couple may or may not do with one another sexually; for example, a couple may only have sex in one position or only one partner may be active during foreplay. Pain medications can also interfere with intimacy.

Carol and Ben
Carol had experienced vertigo migraine headaches for years before she met her husband, Ben. Any movement that would make Carol dizzy could trigger these unwanted headaches. Unfortunately, Ben's movements in bed when they were intimate would sometimes trigger Carol's migraines. Carol did not have much luck controlling her migraines, even with the newest medications. However, Ben was becoming bored with their almost motionless sex life. Losing sympathy, he began turning to pornography. The couple became more and more distant emotionally over time.

Mitch and Fiona
Fiona was becoming increasingly frustrated with Mitch, who developed erectile dysfunction over the course of the five years they had been together. Neither one of them had put together the fact that Mitch's erections were becoming more and more infrequent as the pain in his neck from a traffic accident grew in intensity. A visit to a sex therapist with knowledge about pain disorders helped them to identify that Mitch was in enough pain that he often did not really feel like having sex. However, Mitch did not like to complain or disappoint Fiona. The sex therapist helped the couple to brainstorm some new ways they could have sex with each other, even if that meant that Mitch simply pleased Fiona manually on nights he was too ill for sex. The couple grew to learn that they could still have a sex life, even if it did not look like it once did.

The medications used to treat chronic pain can be problematic when it comes to sex. Some medications are sedatives and cause drowsiness. Others, like antidepressants, can have such sexual side effects as problems with delayed ejaculation and lack of desire. Opioid-type medications like oxycodone can affect a man's production of testosterone, which can lead to problems with erections and low sexual interest.

The location of the pain itself can also create a problem for couples. Having pain in a localized part of the body (e.g., the jaw) may have less of an effect on a couple's sex life than experiencing pain all over or in a joint (e.g., the hip) that affects mobility for sex. The well partner can find a person's pain confusing. They can find themselves so uncertain about whether or not they can touch a partner without hurting them that they stop physical affection altogether.

Larry and Pat

Although Larry was only 55, he had already had his share of chronic problems, including fibromyalgia and diabetes. His wife, Pat, appreciated that Larry did a good job at managing his diabetes, but she found it frustrating that Larry complained that sometimes his pain medication made him too tired for sex. In truth, Larry also felt less like a man since the fibromyalgia diagnosis, only because this disease is much more often found in women. Like some women with fibromyalgia, Larry had experienced childhood abuse. Fortunately for Larry, his marriage to Pat had helped him in large measure to emotionally heal. Still, the disease threatened their intimate life together.

With Pat's encouragement, Larry was able to bring up the problem with his physician, with whom he felt more comfortable talking about such matters. Together with the doctor, Larry was able to adjust his medication so that his pain was still managed but he was alert at the times he and Pat were most likely to have sex. The nurse also suggested ordering some special lovemaking pillows so that Larry could have sex without putting much strain on his joints.

Aside from the physical problems associated with pain disorders, there can also be emotional fallout. Sometimes conditions are such that a person can become temporarily or permanently disabled. They may alter a person's appearance, as with some types of arthritis or surgeries. These can weigh on a partner's self-esteem, making them feel unattractive and undesirable. The well partner can also develop feelings of resentment that undermine a couple's intimate bond.

Couples in which one partner has pain should strive to maintain intimacy. Studies have shown that being physically and emotionally close to a partner can actually help to alleviate pain. In one study, people were given an MRI—generally considered to be an uncomfortable test—under three conditions: alone, holding the hand of a health care person, and holding the hand of their partner. People definitely reported feeling less discomfort when holding their partner's hand. The researchers suggested that real changes in the brain happen when a couple is intimate, such as releasing the natural painkillers known as endorphins. That is why making the effort to be intimate despite the challenge of pain is, for most couples, well worth the effort.

Sexual Pain Disorders

Sexual pain—sometimes also called "pelvic pain" because it is associated with the pelvic floor muscle—is a most frustrating condition when it comes to a couple's intimate life. It is a condition that can affect women and men. Because the sexual anatomy and function is directly affected, a couple's sex life can come to a true standstill. But this need not be the case. Couples in which one partner has sexual pain need to be more patient and creative but no less loving than other couples who do not have this problem.

Sexual pain is caused by many different problems. The following are the most common types of sexual pain disorders:

- *Vaginismus:* Vaginismus is diagnosed when the pelvic floor muscle is so contracted that a woman cannot experience vaginal penetration. Vaginismus can be situational; that is, a woman may be able to insert a tampon but not be able to have intercourse with her male partner. It can also be lifelong or acquired. Vaginismus can leave couples very confused and upset. Many women do not discover that they have vaginismus until the first attempt at intercourse, and it is probably the most common reason that couples sometimes fail to consummate their marriage.
- *Vulvodynia:* This refers to several painful conditions of the vulva, or the tissues that surround the entrance to the vagina. They can be caused by infections, skin conditions, inflammation, or even such neurological problems as damage to the nerves that go to the pelvis, especially the pudendal nerve. The pain can range from mild to excruciating.
- *Dyspareunia:* Dyspareunia, or pain with intercourse, is diagnosed in women when the sexual pain occurs within the vagina, cervix, or other place in the pelvic region during intercourse. It can be caused by insufficient lubrication, changes in hormones because of birth control, menopause, or natural causes, problems like endometriosis, irritable bowel syndrome, treatments like chemotherapy or radiation for cancer, and infections such as pelvic inflammatory disease. Men can have dyspareunia also, either due to pain in the penis and/or testicles after intercourse, or to conditions like those described below.
- *Prostatitis:* This is a condition that can cause men to have painful sex, although the pain can be more generalized (e.g., pain in the lower back or abdomen). Prostatitis can also cause decreased sexual desire and problems with erection.
- *Peyronie's disease:* A man can develop a lump in his penis, along with pain, that eventually causes the penis to bend, sometimes at odd angles. Not only can the condition be painful for the man, but the angle of his penis may also cause pain for his partner.

As with pain disorders due to general medical conditions, there can be emotional factors that interplay with sexual pain disorders. They include psychological problems like anxiety, depression, problems with body image, and relationship problems. Stress can also be a contributing factor because the muscles of the pelvic floor are sensitive to it Finally, although not all women and men with sexual pain have a history of sexual abuse, having had this experience can also play a role in the development of sexual pain problems.

Sexual pain also can be cyclical. A partner with sexual pain will often try to have sex despite the discomfort, which causes bracing for pain. That, in turn, leads to increased pain. After awhile, one or both partners may give up trying to have sex altogether. Sexual pain can cause other strains in the relationship, especially if the partner has unfortunately been told that the pain is "all in your head." This can lead to unnecessary blame and arguing, which can also contribute to increased physical pain.

It is not an understatement to say that sexual pain problems can ruin an intimate relationship if they are not treated correctly. Generally, it "takes a village" or treatment team to treat sexual pain. The team should consist of a physician trained or interested in sexual medicine; a physical therapist; a psychologist or sex therapist; and, if prescribed or desired, adjunctive therapies such as acupuncture. The well partner should be involved in and understand the treatment, which can range from topical medications to hormonal treatment to pelvic floor exercises ("Kegels") and biofeedback.

* * *

Sexual Solutions When the Problem Is Chronic or Sexual Pain

Talking to Your Physician

If you have a chronic illness or pain disorder of any type and it is interfering with your ability to function as an intimate partner, then you need to let your physician know about your struggles. The doctor can help you better manage your condition, make changes in medication in terms of dosing or timing, and suggest ways to have more comfortable sex. Treatments can also sometimes be timed so that you have recovered by the weekend, or whenever you and your partner are more likely to want to have sex. The physician can also prescribe medications for erectile dysfunction, antidepressants for mood and anxiety, and, of course, for pain management. If you feel uncomfortable talking to your physician, consider talking to a nurse in the practice because nurses sometimes have greater interest in quality-of-life issues.

Be aware that pain medications can also have sexual side effects. Antidepressants are now notorious for the possibility of decreasing sex drive and impairing orgasmic function, but antihypertensives (blood-pressure-lowering), statins (cholesterol-lowering), some antipsychotics, and other medications can also cause sexual problems. If you suspect that one or more of your medications are causing sexual side effects, then talk to your physician. Never go off any medication without first consulting your doctor.

Visiting a Health Psychologist

A health psychologist is trained to help people better cope with disease, pain, or both. If you are fortunate enough to find a sex therapist who also has a background in working with people with chronic illness, then that therapist can help you learn such skills as relaxation, changing perspectives and thoughts, planning for ebbs and flow in your energy levels, manage the effect of the illness on your relationships, treat any anxiety or depression related to your illness, and so forth. A health psychologist can be a valuable member of your team when the problem is a pain disorder.

Seek Sex Therapy

Sex therapy can also be important if the pain has been ongoing for a long period of time, because even after treatment, the partner with pain can continue to have an aversion to sex. You also may need help to restore your intimate life together. This can be done with sensate focus activities (see appendix 1) as well as good communication about sex, including sexual wants and needs; timing; approach to initiating sex; and, for some couples, grieving about the sex life they once enjoyed. Sex therapy can also be helpful if childhood abuse is one of the problems that have contributed to the pain.

Some sex therapists also have an interest and training in working with people who have chronic medical conditions. They can help an individual cope better with the demands of such conditions with relaxation, visualization, cognitive psychotherapy (changing one's thoughts and perspective about the condition), and other coping techniques.

Sexual Positions

Switching sexual positions can work for people with nonsexual and sexual pain. For nonsexual pain, the partner with pain can be the passive partner. Sometimes switching positions (e.g., for side entry) can upset a couple's so-called sexual script. It may not seem as erotic if both partners are relatively passive or if one partner or the other is not in their usual dominant position. This is an issue that can be talked through together. It may be that you will need to explore how to make foreplay more erotic and afterplay more worthwhile, with less emphasis put on intercourse.

For a female partner with sexual pain, often the woman on top position is more comfortable because then she can control how much depth of penetration occurs. There are other ways to simulate intercourse that can be used. In a missionary position, a woman can keep her legs closed and the man his legs open so that he can use friction against the woman's inner thighs. It is also possible for a man to use friction between the breasts or the buttocks.

Alternatives to Intercourse

Sometimes couples find that intercourse is not possible. This can be very upsetting because many people feel that only intercourse is "normal sex." Although making a change in thinking might be challenging, doing without sexual stimulation at all is probably an unwelcome situation. Couples with open minds can still have a full sex life by engaging in oral or manual sex. Partners can pleasure each other simultaneously or take turns. One partner can also masturbate to orgasm while being stroked and cuddled if the other partner is too tired to participate.

Vibrators and Lubricants

Sometimes couples feel as if it is "cheating" to use sexual aids, reasoning that if the sexual connection between two partners is good, things like lubricants and sex toys are not necessary. But all kinds of things about people and relationships change over time, including physical changes due to illness, medications, pregnancy, hormonal status, and aging. Admitting that sexual aids could be the answer to having comfortable sex is preferable to deciding that sex is altogether impossible. The issue becomes one of grieving one's former health or hormonal status and embracing the new way of having sex.

Lubricants help when vaginal dryness is an issue. In general, water-based lubricants are recommended because glycerin, an ingredient commonly found in many lubricants, can contribute to an increase in yeast infections. However, if yeast infections have ever been an issue, you can try a silicone-based lubricant instead. Silicone has more "slip" than water-based lubricants and does not need to be reapplied. Some people object to the fact that silicone is a manmade product; for them, there are natural lubricants that are made from ingredients such as carrageen, which comes from seaweed. Also, be sure to use only water-soluble lubricants with latex condoms.

Lubricants are generally thought of as being used for intercourse, but if intercourse is painful or uncomfortable, a lubricant can be used to make manual sex more enjoyable, too.

* * *

BDD

BDD is diagnosed when a person becomes preoccupied with a real or an imagined minor flaw. It affects 1–2 percent of the U.S. population, 90 percent of whom are women, although researchers believe the number of male sufferers may be under reported because of stereotyping. People with BDD will report feeling emotional pain or disgust when they view, perceive, or think about the flaw. The person will have a strong belief that this flaw makes him or her defective, a physical and social reject.

A person with BDD may avoid social situations in which they may be judged on appearance. They also may avoid looking at themselves in mirrors or obsessively look to the point that they may injure themselves (e.g., while looking in the rearview mirror of their car while driving). They may wear makeup or clothing to hide the perceived flaw. They may also undergo cosmetic procedures, which may be common (breast augmentation) or uncommon (contouring the forehead), but they are often dissatisfied with the result and will repeat the surgery to perfectly correct the flaw.

Of course, there is real social pressure in Western society to conform to certain ideals of beauty. Images of good-looking men and women in magazines, film, and television may confuse people into believing that they also should look like a carefully groomed or airbrushed actor or model. Although comparing oneself to an admired role model is not unusual, it is the degree of perfectionism and self-judgment that is alarming. A person with BDD can become so distressed about their appearance that they may talk about amputating a flawed body part or even committing suicide. Clearly, BDD can be a serious disorder that needs treatment.

Julie and Len

By day, few people would notice the blemishes that Julie, age 25, took great pains to carefully cover up. However, they might notice that she wore very thick, masklike makeup that Julie believed hid the "hideous" pale pink marks on her face. The makeup also covered up the flaws only she could see, which in reality were simply the normal pores of her skin.

No amount of reassurance from her high school sweetheart, Len, could convince Julie that there was little wrong with her face. As Julie suffered, so did Len, because Julie would excuse herself from his company at night so that she could spend an hour, or two or three, in the bathroom looking at her face and applying lotions and creams. Although she had been to over a dozen dermatologists who told her that the best thing she could do for her skin was to leave it alone, Julie never listened. Nor did she listen when Len threatened to leave if she kept spending night after night at the mirror.

BDD can be focused on something like a mole, freckle, or acne blemishes; a feature like the nose or hair; or on a part of the body, including breasts and genitals. Any of these can cause a disruption in a couple's love and sex life. However, the relationship between BDD and sexual dysfunction is not exactly understood, except it seems that shame about the body can lead to lack of sexual arousal and pleasure. It appears that men and women with BDD may physically and emotionally "disconnect" from their bodies and the positive feelings that they might get from them.

WHAT CAUSES BDD?

A study published in February 2010 suggests that the brains of sufferers of BDD differ from healthy individuals. Using functional MRI technology while subjects looked at themselves in a mirror, the researchers learned that the left side of the brain, associated with categorization and details, is much more active in sufferers of BDD. Researchers believe that helping people with BDD see their features in a more holistic way may become a part of treatment.

Sex Solutions When the Problem Is BDD

Treatment

The treatment for BDD is a combination of cognitive behavioral therapy and antidepressants. Antidepressants can help the person with BDD obsess less about their flaws. Cognitive behavioral strategies can help them to have a more realistic perspective of their body and to reduce ritualistic behaviors such as checking themselves in the mirror.

Partners of People with BDD

Psychologists recently discovered that people with BDD who are in a relationship are less likely to have diminished sexual pleasure than those who are not. They reasoned that social support helped the person with BDD, and that it might be helpful for the BDD partner to tell their non-BDD partner about their bodily concerns. In return, the non-BDD partner can help the BDD partner by reflecting positive observations about the

BDD partner's body. What is not helpful is to dismiss the BDD concerns as being unrealistic or to make fun of their beliefs. Compassion, patience, and psychological treatment of the BDD individual and, in some cases, of the couple, can be helpful.

Modifications to Sexual Activity

One obvious way to make sex more comfortable when the problem is BDD is to focus more on positive personal qualities, emotions, and sensations than on physical appearance. Allow time for the partner with BDD to relax and get into the appropriate mindset, perhaps by listening to soothing music, taking a walk, or simply talking quietly about sexual positives, such as being able to give and receive pleasure.

Another thought is to make it acceptable for the person with BDD to come to bed with a bit of clothing on. If it makes a woman more relaxed if she wears a camisole or a man to keep on a pair of shorts until he feels comfortable removing them, there is more help than harm. With such acceptance, it is possible that the BDD partner may feel more trust and become a more open sexual partner.

HYPOCHONDRIASIS

Hypochondriasis is a disorder in which a person believes that he or she has symptoms of an undiagnosed disease. No one is certain how many people in the United States have the disorder, but it is thought to affect both sexes equally; estimates are from 0.5 to 8 percent. It is considered to be a somatoform disorder that is psychological in nature; some researchers believe that it is a form of obsessive-compulsive disorder. The person with hypochondriasis will be watchful of any change in the body and may obsessively check for symptoms; for example, taking their temperature or looking inside of the mouth for sores. The person may make repeated visits to physicians for exams or medical testing but frequently does not feel reassured by them.

Sometimes hypochondria can interfere with a person's ability to function in sexual relationships. A person with hypochrondria may worry that they have a sexually transmitted disease (STD) or fear that any sexual contact with their partner will cause an STD, even if their partner has been repeatedly tested. They may worry about problems with fertility, such as whether or not they are ovulating or producing sperm at any moment in time. Sexual dysfunction can also occur; if a man constantly worries about whether or not he will have an erection and constantly seeks reassurance from health care providers, then he may enter into a vicious cycle of hypochondriac-type worry and sexual problems.

WHAT TRIGGERS HYPOCHONDRIASIS?

Hypochondriasis is usually first triggered in young adulthood, although it can happen at any age. Some possible triggers include:

- Media coverage of diseases
- Major disease outbreaks
- Predictions of a pandemic
- Approaching the age at which a parent died prematurely
- A minor medical problem that a person obsesses over
- Depression and panic disorders

Hypochondriasis can cause strain in intimate relationships. The partner with hypochondria can become self-absorbed, focusing all of their energy on ruling out an illness or condition. At the same time, they may constantly check with their partner for reassurance, which can also be wearing. If the symptoms are focused on an illness or dysfunction of a sexual nature, this can have a clear impact on a couple's physical intimacy.

Sexual Solutions When the Problem Is Hypochondriasis

Hypochondriasis can be very difficult to treat. There is some research that shows that a combination of an antidepressant and cognitive therapy can help to alleviate symptoms. Because the person with hypochondriasis may get emotional benefits or "secondary gain" from their reassurance-seeking behavior, couples or family therapy might also be helpful. The nonhypochondriasis partner may need to learn to set boundaries, and the couple may need to communicate clearly and directly about their needs and their emotions.

If the symptoms of hypochondriasis are of a sexual nature, then some sessions with a sex therapist might be in order. The sex therapist can help the person understand their cognitions or thoughts about sex. For example, does the person with hypochondriasis feel guilty or ashamed about sex in some way? Do they feel sexually inadequate? The sex therapist can also help the person understand how and why they might be using their symptoms to manage how emotionally close or distant they are from their partner.

Finally, relaxation and stress management can be helpful for both partners. Massage can be a good way to remind the partner with hypochondriasis that his or her body can function and be a source of healing rather than distress. It can also provide a welcome segue into more sensual activity if such activity always or occasionally provokes anxiety.

RESOURCES

Books

Asmundson, Gordon J. G., and Steven Taylor. *It's Not All in Your Head: How Worrying about Your Health Could Be Making You Sick—and What You Can Do about It*. New York: The Guilford Press, 2005.

Cash, Thomas F. *The Body Image Workbook: An Eight-Step Program for Learning to Like Your Looks*. Oakland, CA: New Harbinger Publications, 2004.

Caudill, Margaret A. *Managing Pain Before It Manages You*. New York: The Guilford Press, 2001.

Claiborn, James, and Cherry Pedrick. *The BDD Workbook: Overcome Body Dysmorphic Disorder and End Body Image Obsessions*. Oakland, CA: New Harbinger Publications, 2002.

Turk, Dennis C., and Frits Winters. *The Pain Survival Guide: How to Reclaim Your Life*. Washington, DC: American Psychological Association, 2005.

Online Resources

American Chronic Pain Association: http://www.theacpa.org/default.aspx.

American Pain Foundation: http://www.painfoundation.org.

International Pelvic Pain Society: http://www.pelvicpain.org.

National Vulvodynia Association: http://www.nva.org.

Patient UK. Health Anxiety—A Self-Help Guide: http://www.patient.co.uk/health/Health-Anxiety-A-Self-Help-Guide.htm.

Chapter Six

EATING DISORDERS

Eating disorders are potentially fatal mental illnesses. Approximately 8 million Americans—7 million women and 1 million men—are believed to have an eating disorder. One in 200 American women has anorexia, which is characterized by an abnormal fear of fat and unnecessary dieting, not to lose weight but to achieve an elusive state of happiness. Another 2–3 American women out of 100 have bulimia, the disorder in which a person takes in an enormous number of calories, only to purge them through vomiting and other means.

Eating disorders are characterized by extremes. Food intake can range from nonexistent to massive; reactions to weight loss or gain can take on catastrophic proportions; and health can teeter because of being extremely under- or overweight. Living with someone who has an eating disorder can be challenging because the partner often observes only these extreme symptoms and naturally focuses concern upon the activity of eating. However, having an eating disorder is more a struggle with feelings toward oneself, one's body, and self-control than about calories and food. It is a struggle that the individual may try to cope with all alone, believing that weight control is the key to self-esteem and identity.

Two types of eating disorders are most frequently diagnosed. One is anorexia nervosa, in which a woman[1] restricts calorie intake through diet, exercise, or both. The other is bulimia nervosa, in which a woman takes in an unusually large number of calories and then purges the intake with vomiting, enemas, laxatives, or diuretics. Women with bulimia nervosa may also abuse diet pills or street drugs like methamphetamine to speed up metabolism. A woman with anorexia can also be diagnosed with bulimia, and a woman with bulimia can become anorexic if her weight drops below 85 percent of expected weight for her age and height.

Eating disorders are complex and can be very serious; people with such disorders have the highest rate of death from suicide of all psychiatric illnesses. In addition, approximately 20 percent of people with eating disorders die, often from heart or kidney disease. Eating disorders most often begin in adolescence but can also occur in later adulthood. Bulimia may especially be triggered later in life by stress. Most sufferers are female: Only approximately 5–15 percent of those with anorexia or bulimia are male, as are approximately 35 percent of binge eaters. The causes are said to be biopsychosocial (i.e., part biological, part psychological) and in part due to the social environment. People with an eating disorder may also have such other psychological diagnoses as anxiety, depression, or substance abuse.

Treating Anorexia and Bulimia

Treating someone with an eating disorder includes the following steps:

- Restoring the person to a healthy weight.
- Treating psychological issues related to the eating disorder (e.g., anxiety, depression, obsessive-compulsive disorder, or trauma).
- Reducing or eliminating thoughts that led to the eating disorder and preventing relapse.

The earlier the diagnosis is made and treated, the better the outcome.

SEX, INTIMACY, AND ANOREXIA NERVOSA

Food and sex are naturally entwined because each drive is biologically regulated in the brain. Those drives are tied to complex feelings and are also affected by a person's social environment. Eating disorders notoriously affect weight, but they are also related to problems with body image, negative emotions like shame and guilt, and struggles over the issue of control of one's own appetites. These problems are similar to those people with a sexual-aversion experience in relation to sexual activities.

Also, like many sexual behaviors, eating disorders are often practiced in secret. Just as someone may hide what gives him or her sexual pleasure, a person diagnosed with an eating disorder may disguise how much they eat or, in the case of bulimia, the aftermath of their food consumption (e.g., hiding food wrappers or frequently wiping down the bathroom after vomiting). The deception required to hide an eating disorder, along with shame, guilt, and low self-esteem, can affect intimacy and sexuality, with low sexual desire, difficulties with arousal, and lack of orgasm being most common.

Part of sexual development is an awareness of one's ability to attract attention and to be desired. For women with anorexia, this process goes awry. Some psychologists believe that the social pressure for women—and, increasingly, men—to be thin and attractive is one of the major causes of eating disorders. Images of women in all different media show an idealized body type that is much thinner than average. Photofinishing techniques also take pounds off and add curves to a woman's body. (The average American woman is 5'4" and wears a size 11–14; the average model is 5'11" and wears size 00–0.) A young teen who is just becoming aware of the power of sexual attraction may become overly self-conscious about her body and attempt to control her weight through starvation, purging, or excessive exercise. There is a great "fear of fat" among people with eating disorders.

Conversely, other theorists have suggested that teens and young women, particularly those with anorexia, are trying to prevent themselves from developing into sexually desirable women. By starving, a female can maintain a body that looks more girlish than womanly—no breasts, no hips, and often no menstruation. Because men are highly visual when it comes to selecting a partner, making oneself the visual opposite of what men are attracted to is one way to covertly reject male attention.

EATING DISORDERS AND FERTILITY

Several groups of researchers have identified that many women who visit infertility clinics—in one study, as high as 17.8 percent—have an eating disorder. Aside from amenorrhea (the suppression of menstruation), eating disorders can affect fertility in the following ways:

- Irregular menstrual cycles, making ovulation erratic and unpredictable
- Reduced egg quality
- Failure of the ovaries to produce eggs
- Miscarriage

The lack of menstruation and development of secondary sex characteristics is indicative of hormonal imbalances that also may decrease a woman's biological sex drive. This delay of menstruation can last for many years after anorexia has gone into remission. In addition, women with anorexia tend to express disgust over the idea of pregnancy and with the physical changes in the female form during pregnancy. It may be one of the reasons they are less likely to marry than are women without anorexia. Women with bulimia can also experience amenorrhea.

Gwen and Matt

The scale read 92 pounds but as Gwen stepped off, her head went into a tailspin. How could she have gained a pound? She berated herself for eating an entire carton of cottage cheese with a single canned peach. She turned and looked at herself sideways in the mirror. Disgusting! Then she caught her husband's pained look in the reflection.

"What? Why are you looking at me?"

"Gwen, I'm worried about you. I married a woman, and you look—." Matt cut himself off.

"I look gross! I gained a ton of weight!"

"You look like a little girl. I don't know what's going on with you. The doctor said you had to start eating if you ever want to get your period so we can have a kid."

"Oh, Matt, the only reason you want to try getting pregnant is to have sex!" Gwen, who never could understand what all the fuss was about sex, also hid the fact that she couldn't stand the thought of being pregnant and looking "deformed."

Matt's jaw fell open as he watched Gwen shove her feet into running shoes for yet another three-hour run to work off all the calories she had eaten that day.

Perfectionism

Researchers have called the Western strong emphasis on physical appearance "self-objectification." When a woman self-objectifies, she thinks of her body as an object to be admired, just as one might admire a piece of sculpture. She can become preoccupied with whether others find her form pleasing or not. Unfortunately, when an intimate partner admires a woman for her slim physique, the partner may unwittingly contribute to a woman's sense of self-worth as an object of beauty: Witness the evolution of the term "trophy wife," a description of a woman attractive enough to dangle on a man's arm like a prize. Many women keep themselves slim in the belief that a good figure is what keeps their husband's fidelity intact.

Eileen and Nelson

Married for 18 years, Eileen struggled to maintain a weight of 102 pounds—her weight when she first met her husband Nelson. Nelson, the CEO of a small oil company, let it be known from the get-go that he would not tolerate a "fat" wife. Eileen, now 53, so feared losing her husband's love if she gained a pound or two that she never became pregnant. She also wanted to be sure she could fit into the expensive designer clothes she had collected over the years. Eileen drank two cans of meal substitute every day and had a dry chicken breast or piece of fish and a salad with lemon every night. For Nelson's part, he had long ago given up on sex with Eileen, who was too worried about her figure to really enjoy it, but at least she looked fit and trim when he took her to social business engagements.

Psychologists speculate that women preoccupied with physical appearance have a difficult time relaxing and focusing on sexual pleasure with and without their partner present. Reaching orgasm requires arousal, but if a woman is thinking unkind things about her body, she may not be able to get turned on. In fact, researchers have found a negative relationship between body image and sexual satisfaction: The more negative a woman's body image, the less likely she is to self-pleasure, have orgasm, or be in a satisfying intimate relationship.

Women with anorexia tend to be compulsive. They feel that they must think or behave according to rigid standards to prevent something bad—gaining weight and all that goes along with it—from happening. Their perfectionism applies to food, weight, and most everything else. They act with constraint because they need a lot of self-control and the ability to numb their feelings of hunger. Along with numbing the physical need for food, they will also numb their need for sex. To override such strong urges takes not just willpower, but also the ability to deny the existence of one's own feelings.

Control

A woman with anorexia does not permit herself to experience the sensual pleasures of eating—or sex. She does what she feels she must to avoid taking anything into her body, whether it is orally with food or vaginally with penetration. She also avoids doing anything that will allow her body to be affected by others; she maintains a rigid boundary around herself, protecting herself psychologically from feelings. The constraint that she uses to control her food intake may also cause a constraint of her sexual responses, leading to difficulty with arousal and orgasm. Conflict about the pleasure of food and the pleasure of sex can cause a woman with anorexia to eschew both.

Although an anorexic partner may say that she wants the experience of being close to another human being, she may not act on this wish because it means giving up control. The need to numb feelings to stay in control counters what is needed to make sex fun, playful, erotic, and gratifying. This great need for control makes it difficult to trust a partner's motives for emotional and sexual intimacy. By locking down all feelings, a woman with anorexia will have difficulty with sexual arousal and may be unable to have orgasm.

Deceit

Another more insidious factor that prevents an anorexic partner from being intimate is the need to be deceitful so as to hide her disorder. Because Western culture in general tends to favor young, very slim females, teens and young women with anorexia sometimes "pass" as normal-weighted. They may keep on just enough weight to put off suspicion about eating habits, or dress in oversized clothing to hide the fact that they are underweight. They may be deceitful about what they do and do not eat by perhaps hiding food in a napkin, avoiding social outings that involve food, or saying they have eaten when in fact they have not. Not wanting to be found out—to be known—may make it difficult for a woman with anorexia to become emotionally intimate with a partner.

Avoidance

Another barrier to intimacy is that the woman with anorexia puts most of her thought, feeling, and energy into her eating disorder. She may have a hard time giving love and, because of shame and low self-esteem, she may also have difficulty receiving love. A partner of a woman with anorexia may also become frustrated because her disorder restricts her choices of social activities. For example, she may decline invitations to gatherings at which there will be large quantities of food. A partner may also be frustrated by expenses associated with the medical problems that come with having anorexia, such as kidney problems, urinary tract infections, abnormal heart rhythm, bone density loss, and infertility.

SEX, INTIMACY, AND BULIMIA NERVOSA

Women with bulimia nervosa may experience chronic feelings of emptiness and fears about being abandoned, feelings that they try to keep stuffed down by impulsively eating large amounts of food. Although almost everyone understands that comfort food can be a good thing in moderation, the woman with bulimia goes to an extreme, sometimes taking in 3,000–4,000 excess calories in a sitting, the equivalent of drinking approximately 10 chocolate milkshakes. Eating too much leads to feelings of self-recrimination, shame, and guilt. Purging is the activity of choice to not only get rid of food and calories, but the negative feelings as well. After a purge, the woman with bulimia may feel temporary relief, but feelings of emptiness soon begin to bother her again, leading her to engage in a "binge-purge cycle."

Emptiness

The emptiness experienced by a woman with bulimia can definitely extend to the feelings connected with romantic or sexual intimacy. For some women with bulimia, no amount of love or reassurance can fill them up. Thus, they may feel chronically alone, with only food to give them comfort. Especially because most women with bulimia are normal-weighted, they are able to keep their behavior secret: If evidence of their bulimia is discovered, or worse, they require a trip to the emergency room or hospital, perhaps because of an imbalance of electrolytes, they will deny it. Like women with anorexia, keeping their relationship with food secret can be more important than real relationships with real people.

Sheila and Cameron

"Why do we always have to make love with the lights off?" Cameron asked. "I'd love to see your beautiful body!"

"What's so beautiful about it?" Sheila pulled the sheets up higher over her shoulders.

"All the curves—I don't know, I just love it."

"Well, I don't!" Sheila exclaimed and rolled over.

"Come on, Sheila, don't be that way. You know I'm just trying to make you feel better about yourself."

Sheila closed her eyes and her mind swirled. Cameron could never understand that a woman who stuffs herself with a big box of candy for lunch every day and drinks a can of warm prune juice every afternoon just does not feel sexy about her body. But then, Cameron could never find out about her binging and purging, it would be too humiliating. Better that he went on believing that she kept herself anywhere near a normal weight by taking a 30-minute walk with him every evening.

Sexual Experiences

Researchers believe that insecurity and emotional dependence lead some women with bulimia to become sexually active earlier and have more sexual partners than women in general. Impulsivity also seems to be a factor. For example, one researcher discusses the fact that such behaviors as purging with laxatives can cause health problems, as can having multiple sex partners, leading the researcher to conclude that women with bulimia are more willing to take risks with their health. Although they seem to be comfortable with sex, often they engage in sex primarily to please their partner and to keep him interested in maintaining a relationship.

Some women with bulimia may have been sexually or emotionally abused, leading to a compromised sense of self and difficulty with regulating emotions. This, in turn, can roller coaster up and down in a fashion similar to that of people with a borderline personality disorder. Research suggests that people who have been sexually abused can become sexualized early. In other words, they become more interested in sex at an earlier age, and in a more mature way, than would be expected at a given age. Combining sexualization with the struggle to control one's impulses, women with bulimia sometimes have more sexual partners than women who do not have bulimia. They are also more likely to take sexual risks and to experience an unwanted pregnancy, sexually transmitted disease, or additional sexual trauma (e.g., through rape or date rape).

Obsession

Like the woman with anorexia, a bulimic woman may be so focused on managing her calorie intake, her feelings about food, and her anxiety about her weight that she shuts out everything else, including her sex drive and her intimate partner. However, sometimes a woman will have an easier time controlling her binge-purge symptoms if she is living with a partner. However, she may still be preoccupied with her weight and appearance to the exclusion of her mate.

SEXUAL SOLUTIONS WHEN THE PROBLEM IS AN EATING DISORDER

Effects of Treatment of Eating Disorders on the Intimate Relationship

In general, the treatment of eating disorders tends to be more long-term and complex. It often involves a multidisciplinary treatment team that can include physicians, psychotherapists, dietitians, and others, such as art therapists and exercise physiologists. For people with anorexia, the treatment may include an initial hospitalization while the patient regains weight, followed by a program to motivate her to maintain and increase weight gain to a satisfactory goal.

The use of antidepressants is indicated in women with bulimia, but not so much with women with anorexia. As noted in chapter 3, antidepressants can have a negative effect on a woman's sex drive, ability to become aroused, and ease of having orgasm. However, for a bulimic woman who also struggles with sexual promiscuity, this effect may initially be helpful. An antidepressant medication is also helpful while a woman learns to use cognitive behavioral therapy to learn how to change her thinking so that her outlook on herself and her self-worth are more positive, helping her to see that she is more than just a machine that metabolizes food and looks sleek.

Low Sexual Desire

Women with eating disorders may be so focused on their weight, food intake, and body image that they lose interest in sex. Low drive also can be compounded if there is a coexisting mood or anxiety problem. Lack of energy and fatigue from excessive dieting or exercise can also contribute to low desire.

However, loss of sexual interest may also have a great deal to do with the need for control, a need that extends beyond weight. Although it may not seem so, the partner with lower desire does have more control, as they often dictate how often the couple will have sex. When the couple does have sex, they may control other factors, such as having the lights off, what body parts may or may not be touched, what positions the couples can be in, and so forth.

One way to cope with a woman's need for control is not to change it but to understand and work with it. A woman and her partner can talk together to identify what will make her feel safe and comfortable enough to have sex. Such a conversation can also help to build a sense of trust between partners, which in turn increases a woman's ability to be more connected emotionally during sex.

Questions such as the following may help:

- When are times of the day, week, or month that you are more likely to feel like having sex?
- What kinds of things can we do together (light candles, take a romantic walk, etc.) to make you feel comfortable enough to have sex?
- Where is the best place to have sex? (Bedroom, shower, another room in the home, etc.)
- How would you like to be approached for sex? (Ask directly, text message, leave a note on the mirror, etc.)
- What things totally turn you off to having sex? (Being grabbed, being approached after a meal, etc.)

The partner of a woman with an eating disorder needs to be aware that there is no cure for an eating order, only management. Having realistic expectations for a partner with an eating disorder can go a long way toward maintaining compassionate understanding and trust, which are essential if a couple is to begin and maintain a close sexual bond.

Coping with Body Image and Shame

Many books and programs have been dedicated to helping women, and to a lesser degree men, overcome bad feelings about their bodies. However, much of the focus on body image and sexuality in academic research is on women who have had breast or a gynecological cancer, such as ovarian cancer, because these illnesses have a direct effect not just on sexual appearance, but also on sexual function. However, for many people, being judgmental about one's body is what starts an eating disorder. In turn, the eating disorder fuels feelings of shame, guilt, and even disgust.

It is important for the partner of a person with an eating disorder not to become overly critical or judgmental, not only in regard to the physique of the person with an eating disorder, but also any aspect of their disorder that increases negative emotions. Making comments about weight loss or gain, or about the shape and size of the body or parts of the body such as breasts or pectoral muscles, even if meant in a positive way, can do more harm than good. Doing so plays into cultural expectations about the shape and tone of the body. It is more important to focus on the person housed within the body than to the body itself and to take loving care of the body to assist it in this task.

Another way to work on making body image less important when it comes to sexuality is to focus on sensation rather than appearance. In other words, both partners can tune in to how other senses, in addition to sight, add to the lovemaking experience. Use music to distract from thinking negatively about the body in action during lovemaking. Add aromatherapy oils like vanilla or rose. You can also touch one another's skin with such different textures as silk and chiffon scarves, faux fur, terry cloth, and so forth.

Many people who have damaged body image discover massage, or nonsexual touch, to be very healing. You may need to search your community to find a masseuse who specializes in providing therapeutic touch for people; ask your doctor or a physical therapist for help in locating such a person. Other practices such as yoga and tai chi can also be helpful because the focus is not so much on improving one's appearance, but on relaxation and stress management. There can also be spiritual benefits to these practices.

Performance Anxiety

As to specific differences between women with anorexia and women with bulimia, women with anorexia tend to dislike their bodies and to see themselves as being sexually unattractive. Women with bulimia tend to have a body image that fluctuates with their weight. If they are normal-weighted, they may actually be able to put aside their negative self-objectification and enjoy sex. When weight goes up or down, they then may become more self-conscious. This self-consciousness has been related to what original sex therapists Masters and Johnson called "spectatoring." When a woman is a spectator during sex, she is focusing more on her sexual performance and appearance than on the sensations she is feeling. She has a real fear that her partner will judge her body negatively. Thus, she may have difficulty becoming aroused and may have trouble reaching orgasm.

In addition to the sensate focus activity described in appendix 1, you might try this unique approach to massage and foreplay. Select a piece of sensual

---

MINDFULNESS, SEX, AND EATING DISORDERS

Mindfulness, a concept from Eastern religions discussed in earlier chapters on depression and anxiety, works to help people stay in the moment. Mindfulness, or staying in the moment, allows people to let go of or manage guilt and shame about the past and fears about the future. When it comes to sex, mindfulness can help someone to stop "mind chatter" and focus on pleasure. Instead of worrying about sexual performance or other troubles, the person tunes into the sensual experience of giving and receiving physical and emotional affection.

Mindfulness is also used in many treatment protocols for eating disorders. In mindful eating, food is consumed without judgment of the food itself or the act of eating. The focus is on sustenance, health, and pleasure rather than eating the "right" food. The food is savored with all of the senses, and food intake is directed by focusing on natural cues of hunger. Although learning to practice mindfulness takes time, many people find it an invaluable tool for making positive changes.

---

music to enjoy and have some massage oil on hand. Plan to spend approximately 10 minutes taking turns massaging one another to the music. The twist is to pretend that your partner's body is an instrument to be played. How might your strokes and firmness of touch change to the beat and feeling of the music? By getting lost in the music and the activity of massage, you may find it is easier to let go of how the body looks and focus more on how it feels.

NOTE

1. The gendered term "woman" will be used in this and in most sections of this chapter because 90 percent of sufferers of eating disorders are female, and most of the current research on the topic is centered on women.

RESOURCES

Books

Morgan, John F. *The Invisible Man: A Self-Help Guide for Men with Eating Disorders, Compulsive Exercise, and Bigorexia.* New York: Routledge, 2008.

Ross, Carolyn Coker. *The Binge Eating & Compulsive Overeating Workbook: An Integrated Approach to Overcoming Disordered Eating.* Oakland, CA: New Harbinger Publications, 2009.

Sacker, Ira M., and Marc A. Zimmer. *Dying to be Thin: Understanding and Defeating Anorexia Nervosa and Bulimia—A Practical Lifesaving Guide.* New York: Grand Central Publishing, 1987.

Siegel, Michele, Judith Brisman, and Margot Weinshel. *Surviving an Eating Disorder, Third Edition: Strategies for Family and Friends.* New York: Harper Paperbacks, 2009.

Online Resources

Medline Plus: Eating Disorders: http://www.nlm.nih.gov/medlineplus/eatingdisorders.html.

National Association of Anorexia and Associated Eating Disorders: http://www.anad.org.

National Eating Disorders Association: http://www.nationaleatingdisorders.org.

Chapter Seven

SUBSTANCE-RELATED DISORDERS

Drug addiction is a brain disease characterized by drug craving, seeking, and using even in the face of dire consequences. Although initial use may be voluntary, scientists have learned that over time, drugs change brain circuitry and even the expression of genes. A user of drugs or alcohol can abuse the substance, meaning that they use the substance inappropriately to derive some benefit such as relaxation, to lift their mood, or to decrease anxiety. With prolonged use, they may also become dependent or addicted. Once addiction develops, the individual loses control over the ability to make voluntary choices regarding drug use. All drugs (including alcohol) are potentially harmful and may become life-threatening.

Drug and alcohol addiction are, unfortunately, relatively common mental disorders. For alcohol alone, estimates are that 1 in 12 adults in the United States abuse alcohol or are alcohol-dependent. But demographics shift depending on the age, type of drug use, and other characteristics of a population. For example, although there has been a small decline in the number of teens abusing alcohol and street drugs, the number of who abuse prescription drugs such as Xanax and OxyContin has increased over the past 10 years. Meanwhile, during the same decade, the number of baby boomers abusing substances has doubled. However, overall, people from every walk of life, from every age, race, and religion, abuse substances.

When one or both partners abuse potentially dangerous substances as alcohol, street drugs, or potentially addictive prescription medications, the results can be personal and interpersonal chaos. Over time, substance abuse and dependence can cause physical damage, but it can also alter one's mental and psychological state enough to threaten or destroy intimate emotional and sexual connections. When substance use becomes chronic, a partner may spend more time thinking about, acquiring, and using a substance than they do about almost anything else, including the people who love them.

People commonly turn to alcohol and drugs to escape uncomfortable feelings. Because substances do not discriminate between feelings, all emotions become numbed; along with fear and depression, love and desire are also affected. That is part of the reason why sexuality is an aspect of intimacy that can be affected by substance abuse or dependence. It is ironic that alcohol and some other substances can initially have a positive effect. For example, alcohol may help a person relax enough to initiate or overcome sexual inhibitions, or a man might use cocaine before sexual activity because it makes him feel masculine and sexually powerful. A woman might drink because it makes her flirtatious and able to attract male attention, which increases her self-esteem, at least temporarily.

But when it comes to substances, there can definitely be too much of a good thing. Although moderate use provides a performance boost, at some point, the more substance used, the less satisfying the sex. Because different types of substances can cause different effects on the brain and central nervous system, they can also cause different types of sexual dysfunction, all of which will be discussed in this chapter.

HOW SUBSTANCES AFFECT SEXUAL FUNCTION

It is not unusual for someone, male or female, to turn to alcohol or drugs to enhance sexual performance or to overcome fears related to sex and intimacy. Although a little bit of alcohol—an ounce for women, two ounces for men—may help someone to relax and enjoy sex, too much alcohol can get in the way. (An ounce of alcohol equals one shot of hard liquor, one 6-ounce glass of wine, or one 12-ounce beer.) The same is true for other street and prescription drugs.

Jeffrey

Jeffrey always had a problem with premature ejaculation. In fact, at times when he was with a partner, he was so nervous about whether or not he would be able to last long enough to satisfy her that he would ejaculate before he had even undressed. However, he noticed a pattern: If he had enough to drink, he could successfully have intercourse and even last a good five minutes—sometimes more. Jeffrey figured the alcohol calmed him down, and soon he became dependent on it not only to gain self-control, but also to make him feel more desirable. That worked until one night he discovered he could not ejaculate at all, which embarrassed him almost as much as ejaculating too soon. Soon Jeffrey was drinking enough to pass out, avoiding sex with his partner altogether.

There are many men like Jeffrey whose ability to perform becomes negatively affected by drinking. Some men may not realize that alcohol is affecting their ability to get aroused and maintain an erection. This can lead to self-blame, which in turn can lead to more substance abuse, creating a vicious cycle. Eventually, a man can feel so ashamed of his sexual "weakness" that recovery becomes difficult.

Research does suggest that feelings of sexual inadequacy can contribute to problem alcohol and drug use. In one study of 61 men in recovery for substance abuse, 75 percent reported having sexual problems before beginning the use of drugs, including premature ejaculation, premature ejaculation with erectile dysfunction (ED), and low desire. Approximately 30 percent of those men said that their sexual problems influenced their decision to use drugs.

Women also may use alcohol as a "medication" to help them feel more sexual pleasure and less sexual distress. Those who abuse alcohol in this way may be reluctant to give up drinking and to have sex sober. The prospect of making love without being under the influence can be frightening enough that a woman who abuses alcohol or becomes alcohol dependent may avoid sex altogether once sobriety is achieved.

In addition, alcohol affects women differently than it does men. Women become more impaired than men do after drinking the same amount of alcohol, even when differences in body weight are taken into account. This is because women's bodies have less water than men's bodies, so that a given amount of alcohol will become more concentrated in a woman's body than a man's. Additionally, alcohol addiction takes a heavier toll on women than men: Problems such as brain, heart, and liver damage also progress more rapidly.

Gay, lesbian, bisexual, and transgender people may drink to numb the painful emotional effects of personal and social consequences (e.g., difficulties with isolation, anxiety, and anger) associated with their sexual orientation. They may feel that they need to drink to quell negative, homophobic messages so that they can engage in sex with a person of the same sex. In addition, claiming to be under the influence during a same-sex sexual encounter can also be used

---

MOTIVATING A PARTNER TO GET HELP

What can you do if your partner is abusing or is dependent on drugs or alcohol? One thing is certain: You cannot force someone to stop using substances. However, you can take certain steps to help your partner get treatment.

- Stop covering up or protecting your partner from the consequences of his or her drinking.
- Time your request after your partner has had a serious problem related to substance use, such as blacking out or getting into an accident. Choose a time when your partner is sober, you are both calm, and you have privacy.

- Be specific and give your partner examples about why he or she needs to stop.
- Tell your partner the consequences if they do not get help, from not attending social events with him or her if substances will be available to moving out. State only consequences that you are prepared to carry out.
- Get help. Do your research on treatment options beforehand. Be prepared to make an immediate appointment.
- Consider a group intervention, in which other family members and friends confront the substance user. Do so only under the guidance of a professional who is trained in this type of intervention.
- Get support. There are support groups for spouses of people who are addicted to alcohol and drugs. Most spouses find Al-Anon and Narc-Anon to be helpful in coping.

Because most substances disinhibit behavior, their use can cause someone to act out sexually or cause someone to be the recipient of unwanted sexual advances. Upon becoming sober, a person may feel a great deal of guilt and shame over past sexual experiences, leading them to become sexually avoidant. If the past sexual acting-out behavior is not acknowledged or addressed, it can create an unintentional divide in a person's current intimate relationship.

---

as a rationalization for behavior someone finds shameful. Although the exact prevalence is unknown, researchers believe that GLBT individuals are more likely than straight individuals to abuse alcohol and substances.

SUBSTANCE ADDICTION, TREATMENT, AND SEXUALITY

Sexual problems can trigger relapses regarding substances an individual is trying to quit, but they often go unaddressed in treatment. As often happens when it comes to sex, well-meaning treatment professionals believe that once the substance abuse is resolved, the sexual problem will take care of itself. However, the fact is that couples who have struggled in the bedroom because of substance abuse by one or both partners can be afraid to restart their intimate relationship. If a woman is used to turning down her partner because of alcohol-tinged breath, or if a man has been losing his erections because of smoking cigarettes, it can take time to change attitudes and behaviors. More seriously, couples in recovery often have to deal with issues of broken trust, abandonment, and arguments over substance abuse, enabling, and codependency, which also may need to be healed if a couple is to be sexually intimate again.

About half of people who enter rehabilitation treatment for substance abuse are thought to have experienced some type of childhood sexual or physical abuse. One researcher discovered that in the group she studied, the younger the male was when the childhood physical or sexual abuse took place, the more significant the substance problem. For women, the age at which the abuse took place did not matter as much as the fact that it happened. In addition, having been traumatized can also influence the quality of one's interpersonal relationships, making intimate connections difficult. Isolation, shame, and low self-esteem can also be an outcome of having been abused. All of these factors can contribute to problems in the bedroom and to substance abuse relapse.

Rita and Hugh

A male babysitter had molested Rita when she was 10 years old, so she pretended she never wanted to hear anything about sex while in her teens. However, when she was away at college, she went to her share of parties and began to drink. Rita liked the way alcohol made her feel, a bit out of control and sexually attractive. She liked the way alcohol warmed her body, including her genitals. Rita's first sexual experience was not a good one: She was drunk and let a fellow student take her back to his room during a party, where he easily forced her onto the sofa for intercourse.

After that, Rita decided she would only drink if she were in a more controlled situation, which for her meant on a date. By the time she met her future husband, it seemed quite normal to down several cocktails before sex. But as the frequency of their sexual activity increased, Rita realized that she could not continue to drink before sex. However, sex without a drink was very uncomfortable for Rita, so much so that she went back to her old drinking habits.

Over time, Rita's drinking escalated. She became mean toward Hugh, yelling accusations that he wasn't fit to be a husband because he didn't earn enough or didn't please her in bed. She blacked out several times and couldn't remember their arguments. Hugh begged her to get help, but it took a DUI for Rita to realize that she had a problem. With help from a rehabilitation counselor, Rita made the connection between the molestation, her bad feelings about sex, and her alcoholism. She hoped Hugh would understand, and that he would agree to attend couples counseling so they could put their marriage back together.

It can be important to wait through several months of sober living to determine the exact effect of the drug on the person's own state of mind regarding sex. For example, a man who is in early stages of alcoholism when he enters sobriety may find that his ability to have an erection improves after a few weeks. Someone in later stages of alcoholism who incurs liver damage may not recover sexual function without the help of sex therapy and sexual medications such as Viagra.

SEXUAL SIDE EFFECTS OF SPECIFIC SUBSTANCES

Various substances affect sexual function in different ways. Some people may find their sexual function is the first to go as their substance use increases, whereas others find it little affected. In this section, I have summarized some of those effects.

Alcohol

Alcohol acts as a disinhibitor in the brain, loosening up a person's behavior. As more alcohol is used, the brain and nervous system become depressed.

Reflexes do not work as well and blood vessels become dilated. This can lead a man to have difficulty achieving an erection or impair a woman's ability to respond sexually, as demonstrated by research suggesting a lack of vaginal lubrication in females with alcoholism. Men may also use this depressive effect to what appears to be a beneficial side effect: It can delay ejaculation, leading them to believe that they are better satisfying the sexual needs of their partner. This is misguided thinking, because over several years, chronic alcohol use can become toxic to the liver, making it difficult for a man's body to produce testosterone. This in turn can lead to poor-quality erections, low sex drive, and what researchers call "feminization syndrome," which includes not just ED but also shrinking of the testicles and development of male breast tissue (gynecomastia). Even after years of sobriety, a chronic alcohol user may not recover his sexual function, which may be due to permanent changes in the brain.

If past childhood abuse or other negative sexual events have contributed to alcoholism, it is possible that treatment will stir up thoughts, memories, and feelings about those incidents. It is not unusual for a person to remember past sexual acting out. There can be deep shame and anger upon the discovery of these types of events that can lead to the avoidance of sex. This can be confusing for both partners, especially if it is not accurately identified and explored in treatment and between partners.

Alcohol can cause women to experience a slight increase in testosterone, which may permit them to be more sexually aggressive than is considered socially acceptable. As it is, women often hide their true level of sexual interest, and drinking allows it to be displayed. In fact, it may be the only time that some women express their drive. Sometimes partners of women who express themselves freely sexually while under the influence are disappointed when that woman cuts back or stops drinking alcohol. Women can have similar performance fears that men do, worrying about how they will respond to a partner when sober.

Unlike men, women's self-report of their arousal does not match up with what is happening physically to their bodies. As women drink, they report becoming more aroused, but measures of physiological response show fewer signs of sexual arousal. It may be that women interpret the alcohol-induced physical effects as sexual arousal, or it may be that women expect alcohol to make them feel more aroused, and so they are.

Like men, women who are alcoholic have significantly higher rates of sexual dysfunction than do nonalcoholic women. One study suggests women that abuse alcohol are at greater risk of continued alcoholism if they have sexual problems. Another issue is that a woman's partner may offer her alcohol to stimulate a stronger interest in sex.

Sometimes both partners abuse alcohol. If they are used to making alcohol a part of their "sexual script," then making love while sober can be very difficult if they both go into treatment or agree not to drink. The drinking behavior may have covered up feelings of sexual inadequacy for both partners. Having to face their fears head-on can lead to avoidance of sexual activity.

Marijuana and Hashish

Like alcohol and other substances, people may use cannabis in various forms to add to their sexual experience. Cannabis-derived drugs such as marijuana and hashish are in a class of their own because they are not considered to be a stimulant, depressant, or hallucinogen. Some of the sexual side effects of marijuana and hashish can be subtle because they can take a long time to develop, whereas others are more immediate. Smoking marijuana can increase sexual interest and enhance erotic thoughts and feelings. It can alter perceptions so that sensory experiences like touch during lovemaking seem to be more intense. Marijuana causes relaxation and a letting go of inhibitions. This may add to a sense of increased emotional closeness, which can be problematic when use is stopped and one or both partners find that their intimacy has been based on a drug-induced experience.

Unfortunately, marijuana also has some negative side effects. Among them are slowed thinking, problems with memory, respiratory problems, increased heart rate, anxiety, and panic, none of which contribute to a better sexual experience. Over time, a user can develop tolerance to the effects of marijuana, which means that they need to spend more time acquiring and smoking it to get the desired effect. While a person is under its influence or "stoned," they may prefer to passively enjoy their high and avoid negative feelings, including worries about sexual performance, rather than participate in social conversation or other activities.

Abe and Jan

Although Abe and Jan dated for two years before moving in together, Jan had no idea how frequently Abe smoked marijuana. But Jan rationalized that Abe smoking marijuana every night after work was similar to someone having a beer and left Abe alone. However, over the years, Abe's marijuana use increased. He smoked first thing in the morning, smoked most of the weekend and, Jan discovered, during his breaks at work. But Abe was successful in his tile-regrouting business, so Jan figured that the marijuana was not having any effect on his ability to function. Nor did Jan realize that Abe's decreasing interest in sex and lack of erection when they tried was related in any way to his smoking.

It was only when Abe visited a urologist and admitted his chronic use of marijuana that he decided to stop smoking. In addition to affecting his testosterone levels, the urologist also said that there was some research suggesting that chronic marijuana might affect sperm health. Knowing that Jan wanted to have children someday, Abe decided to cut way back on his marijuana use.

For men, tetrahydrocannabinol (THC), the active ingredient in marijuana, can also cause a decline in testosterone, which can decrease sexual desire and erectile function. THC can also affect fertility for men and women. In men, it can cause a drop in the volume of semen, a decline in the number of sperm, and a decrease sperm motility (i.e., the ability of the sperm to swim to the egg). In women, THC may be stored in the tissues of the cervix and within vaginal lubrication, which can also interfere with the sperm's journey to fertilize the egg. THC can also disrupt a woman's ovulation and menstrual cycle.

Stimulants

Stimulants such as cocaine and methamphetamine can give a person a surge of energy, mental alertness, and exhilaration that can enhance a sexual experience. However, these substances are highly addictive, excessive use can cause extensive physical damage, such as heart problems, high blood pressure, respiratory distress, and liver damage. From a psychological standpoint, users of amphetamines can become irritable, anxious, impulsive, and aggressive. These side effects, as well as the time and attention an amphetamine addict devotes to acquiring and using the drug, can undermine an intimate relationship on multiple levels.

As for specific sexual side effects, amphetamines can initially increase sexual desire and activity. However, such amphetamines as cocaine can cause a feeling of dullness in the genitals, leading to delayed orgasm for men and women. As with alcohol, for men this may appear to be a benefit, but as the dose and addiction increase, orgasm becomes further delayed, which can lead to frustration and avoidance of sexual activity. Conversely, because of increased excitability, men who use cocaine may also experience premature ejaculation.

Barbiturates

This class of drugs includes prescription medications such as Ambutal, Nembutal, and Seconal. Common recreational effects are relaxation and a feeling of contentment, whereas negative effects include physical and psychological dependence, respiratory problems, ataxia (problems with balance), and death if overdosed. Barbiturates are occasionally prescribed to decrease sexual performance anxiety; other positive sexual effects that people ascribe to barbiturates, such as feeling more sensual, are probably more psychological than chemical. However, barbiturates are highly addictive, and being with a partner who is mentally and emotionally absent because of their abuse can greatly interfere with intimacy.

Nicotine

The physical effects of nicotine—respiratory problems, heart problems, and cancer—have been well studied. Less publicized are the effects of nicotine on sexual function. Men who smoke on a daily basis are at risk for problems including lack of sexual arousal and poor quality of erections. In women, use of nicotine can lead to vaginal dryness, a decrease in the number of eggs, and disruptions in the menstrual cycle, all of which can also affect fertility.

Matt and Bonnie

Married for eight years, 48-year-old Matt began having more and more problems with his erections. Bonnie, somewhat overweight and never very secure about her sexual attractiveness, was patient at first but began taking it personally. She even accused Matt of having an affair, his ED a result of having satisfied himself with another woman. That was the last straw for Matt, who made an appointment with a urologist.

As Matt filled out the intake, he saw a check-off box for smoking tobacco. A smoker since age 13, Matt checked the box and wondered what smoking had to do with urology. But in his exam with the physician, Matt was shocked to learn his smoking habit had almost everything to do with his erections. In fact, nicotine had done so much damage to the vascular system that he was told the only way he would be able to achieve an erection would be with a surgically implanted prosthesis. Although he found an answer, Matt was angry that no one had ever spoken about this serious side effect of nicotine addiction.

Nicotine also can affect a couple's level of intimacy in subtle ways. For example, a nonsmoker may dislike the smell of cigarettes on a partner's breath or clothing. These days, with so many restrictions on where one can smoke, there can be times when the couple cannot be together socially, or the nonsmoker may require the smoker to smoke only outside of the home.

Opioids

Opioids include such highly addictive drugs as heroin, codeine, morphine, and the powerful prescription drug oxycodone. The street and legal forms of these drugs are painkillers that lead to drowsiness, sedation, mental confusion, and euphoria. The euphoric effect can initially enhance sexual activity, but over time, men will experience a decrease of testosterone, along with ED and loss of sexual interest. Women who use opioids also lose sexual interest, but to a lesser extent. In addition, opioids can affect the menstrual cycle and fertility.

Hallucinogens

Hallucinogens include LSD (lysergic acid diethylamide), mescaline, and psilocybin. Some street drug experts also include MDMA

(3, 4-methylenedioxymethamphetamine, or ecstasy) in this class of drugs, (although others classify it as a stimulant). Hallucinogens may heighten the senses and alter the perception of time and space, enhancing the sexual experience. However, they can also cause nervousness and paranoia that can interfere with sexual enjoyment.

WHAT ABOUT SEX ADDICTION?

Is it possible to be addicted to sex, especially Internet pornography? "Sex addiction" may be a popular media term, but you will not find it in the DSM. Although some researchers and addiction specialists are convinced that compulsively seeking out and using pornography causes the same brain changes as substances like cocaine, others remain skeptical. They believe that calling someone a "sex addict" is a hysterical reaction to pornography and sexual activity.

While the experts hash out the question of whether sex can be addictive, there is no doubt that some people are bothered by their own or their partner's use of pornography. In general, if the person's use of pornography interferes with their relationships or their work, then most mental health professionals would consider it a problem. A good psychological assessment can determine what is driving the compulsive use of porn (e.g., a mood disorder, anxiety disorder, relationship, or other problem) and treat it accordingly. A sexual history can also help someone put their own ideas and beliefs about sexuality into a healthier perspective.

SEXUAL SOLUTIONS WHEN THE PROBLEM IS ADDICTION

Sexual History

An addictions specialist or sex therapist familiar with addictions can take a good sexual and relationship history, which can be critical to recovery. This is especially true if the substance user has a history of being sexually abused. But even relatively minor problems can build into bigger issues over time because a person's self-esteem suffers with sexual dysfunction such as premature ejaculation, ED, and anorgasmia. These problems can contribute to substance use and interfere with maintenance of sobriety.

Being willing to accept and face sexual problems that may be at the heart of substance problems takes courage. After all, it is often embarrassment about sex that leads to using alcohol or drugs as a crutch in the first place. The nonaddicted partner needs to give empathy and support while also being willing to work on any sexual problems together with as little blame as possible.

Just because you or your partner has acknowledged that drinking or other substance abuse has been masking a sexual problem does not necessarily mean the problem will go away once sobriety is achieved. For men, erection and ejaculatory control may not improve, and orgasm might be more difficult for women. One of the first steps to take might be to talk to a physician. Although many sexual problems are psychological, there can be physical reasons (including hormonal imbalances) that can interfere with sexual function.

Because substance use "masks" problems, honesty with oneself and one's partner is very important. Letting a partner know that one of the reasons you have had a problem with sobriety is that you do not feel that confident in the bedroom, or that you have inhibitions or hang-ups about sex, is better than hiding them, which can create a vicious cycle. There may be a risk that your partner will be upset by this revelation. For example, a male partner might find it distressing to learn that his female partner cannot achieve orgasm unless they are under the influence.

Keep things in perspective. Although they might be embarrassing, most sexual problems are solvable. You can even have fun trying to solve them. Gather good information, seek counseling if needed, and go slowly. Have a realistic expectation for good sex, not fireworks, not only to keep the relationship, but also to maintain sobriety.

Intimacy After Sobriety

As most anyone who has attended a 12-step meeting knows, the so-called "Big Book" suggests that a person refrain from being in a relationship for a year after sobriety is first achieved. In part, that is because the newly sober person needs to put a lot of energy into staying sober. They might even seem self-absorbed as they develop new ways of coping with life while sober; they may spend more time at 12-step meetings and in therapy than with loved ones.

Of course, if a person is already in a relationship, a one-year waiting period may be impossible. In that case, both partners should proceed slowly with re establishing an intimate connection, with realistic expectations about their intimate relationship as sobriety continues. When the nonrecovering partner discovers that sobriety is not the bed of roses he or she dreamed of, disappointment may ensue. For example, he or she may feel left out of and resent recovery-related activities in which the recovering partner must participate, whereas the newly sober partner may begin to identify relationship dynamics that fed the addiction.

Partners need to expect changes in their relationship. Therefore, it is important for both partners to think and behave as if in they are in recovery, healing from a difficult time and discovering more about who they are and what their relationship stands for if alcohol or drugs are out of the picture. The sober partner should consider going to Al-Anon or a comparable 12-step group geared to help family members and friends of those in recovery to get support from others in the same position and to be able to appropriately support the newly sober partner.

Sex After Sobriety

Once sobriety has been achieved, there may be a desire for one or both partners to "get back to normal" by having sex. The rush to the bedroom can be a mistake because the newly sober partner may be grappling with all kinds of thoughts and feelings about sex and intimacy. In addition, because so many people who abuse substances have faced physical and sexual abuse, it may be difficult for them to handle having sex sober. Couples should take their time to talk and cuddle before attempting to be sexually intimate, allowing both partners the opportunity to sort through such issues as resentment, feeling exploited, or the inability to be assertive when it comes to sex.

A sex therapist may not be the first resource people consider once both partners are sober, but if sexual problems or abuse were factors that contributed to substance use, a sex therapist can help the couple sort things out. Another possibility would be to work with a therapist who is familiar with the fallout of sexual abuse.

Anticipate Changes

What a person enjoys during sex while under the influence may be different than what a person enjoys while sober. A partner who has an "anything goes" attitude while using substances may not only feel more inhibited while sober, but they may also feel ashamed of freewheeling sexual behavior. The sober partner may also be disappointed that sex becomes less exciting than it was with a partner under the influence. However, with time and patience, many people find that sex actually feels better while sober. The body is designed to experience pleasure, so when the effect of substances is removed, the senses are more aware and awake. Not all changes are negative!

Sexual Confidence

If substances have been part of the picture because they help a person perform sexually, then building sexual confidence will be especially important. It is essential to develop and hold positive thoughts and ideas about yourself as a sexual being and partner. The type of positive thoughts you might use to replace negative ones include:

- I feel good about my body.
- I believe I am capable of being a good sexual partner without alcohol or drugs.

- I can tolerate sober sex; I can get used to being intimate with someone without being high.
- I can be a perfectly good lover without being perfect.
- I have the courage to face whatever bothers me about sex and to do something about it.

Sexual confidence is something that builds over time, but generally becomes second nature. It also helps if both partners are patient. Like sobriety, take sexual healing one day at a time.

RESOURCES

Books

Beattie, Melody. *Codependent No More: How to Stop Controlling Others and Start Caring for Yourself.* Center City, MN: Hazelden Publishing, 1992.

Covington, Stephanie S. *A Woman's Way through the Twelve Steps Workbook.* Center City, MN: Hazelden Publishing, 2000.

Kettelhack, Guy. *First Year Sobriety: When All That Changes Is Everything.* Center City, MN: Hazelden Publishing, 1998.

Online Resources

Al-Anon: http://www.al-anon.alateen.org.

Alcoholics Anonymous: http://www.aa.org.

Narcotics Anonymous: http://www.na.org.

Nar-Anon: http://www.nar-anon.org.

National Council on Alcoholism and Drug Dependence: http://www.ncadd.org.

U.S. Government Substance Abuse and Mental Health Services Administration: http://www.samhsa.gov.

Chapter Eight

PERSONALITY PROBLEMS

"Personality" refers to the way we behave that makes us individuals, including how we think, feel, or act. Some personality characteristics are very common, such as being shy, impeccable, dramatic, or proud. These qualities are generally not problematic. However, people can also have these traits to an extreme, such as being shy enough that they avoid social contact or dramatic enough that they are difficult to be around.

When a person meets the criteria for any of the 10 personality disorders (PDs) listed in the DSM, they may find it hard to get along with coworkers, interact with family or friends, or control their own feelings or behaviors. They themselves may become unhappy or make others upset or cause them emotional trouble. Often the person with a PD has difficulty recognizing it, making it a challenge to understand why and how one's own personality might need to change; thus, people with PD tend to blame others for problems. Because having a PD can make life difficult, it can lead to depression, anxiety, or problems like addictions or eating disorders.

To be diagnosed with PD, a person needs to demonstrate two of the following four patterns:

1. A certain, rigid way of thinking about themselves, others, and events
2. A particular range of emotion, which may range from narrow to dramatic
3. Difficulty with interpersonal functioning
4. Problems with impulse control

The personality patterns must also cause the person distress or impairment in social, occupational, or other areas of functioning. Personality problems come to the surface most often when a person is under stress. They are caused by many different factors, including disruptions in attachment to parent figures, child abuse and neglect, overly anxious parenting, the person's temperament, and even genetics.

In terms of committed relationships, PDs can challenge intimate satisfaction. Especially when under duress, the PD partner can be rigid, demanding, self-absorbed, and even manipulative as they blame the non-PD partner for their dissatisfaction. On the other hand, a good partnership requires a charitable view of one's partner, flexibility, and the ability to problem-solve, including problems related to sexual needs and activity. As American psychologist Albert Ellis said, "How you do anything is how you do everything," so if a partner's personality creates problems outside of the bedroom, chances are those same characteristics are also playing out in the bedroom.

There are 10 PDs listed in the current DSM, and these are organized into three "clusters."

1. *Cluster A:* Odd and eccentric personalities, including paranoid, schizoid, and schizotypal PDs
2. *Cluster B:* Dramatic and emotional personalities, including antisocial, borderline, histrionic, and narcissistic PDs
3. *Cluster C:* Anxious or fearful personalities, including avoidant, dependent, and obsessive-compulsive disorders

There is also a classification referred to as "not otherwise specified" (NOS), which is diagnosed when a person has features of more than one PD ("mixed personality"). It is also possible to have traits or features of a PD that can make being in a relationship more difficult without having a full diagnosis.

Although some people argue against labeling anyone with a PD, understanding a PD can often help individuals learn more adaptive ways of coping with various life stressors. It can also help to know that the way a person with a PD has acted is due to a mental illness and may be beyond their control without help with new ways of thinking, acting, and feeling. For example, if one partner sees their partner with obsessive-compulsive personality disorder as someone whose need for control is a defense instead of a weapon, it is easier to have compassion for them and to work toward appropriate solutions to problematic behaviors.

It is unwise to diagnose yourself or someone else on the basis of the brief descriptions in this chapter. Many people have traits of a particular personality, but they function pretty well in their relationships and at work. In addition, other such factors as physical and hormonal health (e.g., thyroid diseases) can affect the way one copes. It takes a mental health clinician—psychiatrist, psychologist, marriage therapist, or social worker—to diagnose the presence of a true disorder.

PDs AND INTIMACY

PDs can be difficult to detect if a person is doing well. A person with PD who is under little stress and is functioning well may appear to have an average personality. Because all intimate relationships by their very nature are bound to be stressful at times, the PD may become apparent only later, sometimes after the loss of a job or the birth of a child. Marriage itself may be enough of a stressor to increase the symptoms of a PD.

In treating a PD, the person with PD needs to first accept that the way in which they are coping and reacting to life stressors, including relationship problems, is not working and that some changes are in order. Then they must be motivated to attend therapy, individually or as part of a couple, to learn how to handle life's challenges in a more flexible and meaningful way.

Couples will essentially need to understand the PD and learn to emotionally detach from its effects. The essential steps in maintaining an intimate relationship when one—or both—partners has a PD include understanding interactions that are most likely to trigger ingrained responses, learning alternative ways of interacting to avoid those triggers as much as possible, and creating an environment in which couples listen and thoughtfully respond to one another rather than reacting.

In general, people with a Cluster B PD are more likely to act out sexually, whereas most with a Cluster C PD will be sexually inhibited. Those with a Cluster A PD are generally loners and are often observed as asexual. Because people with Cluster B and C personality types are more common in the population and more likely to be in a long-term marriage or relationship, the focus of this chapter will be the effects of those PDs on sex and intimacy, followed by suggestions for couples in which one partner has a diagnosed PD.

CLUSTER B: DRAMATIC AND EMOTIONAL PDs

Borderline Personality Disorder

Because people with a borderline personality disorder (BPD) have an unstable sense of self and others, living with and loving someone with BPD can be very difficult. Couples' therapists estimate that approximately half of the couples seen in treatment have one partner who meets at least three of the criteria for BPD. People with BPD think so poorly of themselves that they are certain those they love will abandon them. This possibility makes them frantic, causing them to act out in chaotic ways. They also find it hard to regulate their emotions, so that they may appear moody, even changing from one hour to the next. They may seem to desperately need their partner one moment and hold them in contempt the next. They tend to be dramatic, impulsive, and can be prone to making suicidal gestures and self-mutilation (e.g., "cutting"). Nearly as many men are thought to have BPD as women, but women tend to get diagnosed more often, perhaps because they tend to more theatrically act out their moods and impulses.

Some research suggests that child abuse or such experiences as sexual assault or date rape may contribute to the development of BPD. As a reaction to trauma, a BPD partner may become sexually unstable, either avoiding sex or having multiple casual sexual partners. If they enter into a long-term relationship, often one of two things happens: They may have such sexual problems as feeling physically numb and unable to have orgasm, or they may be hypersexual and dissatisfied with their partner's lack of sexual aggression.

A lack of impulse control and an emotional need to avoid feelings of emptiness can also lead people with BPD to have more sexual experiences than others. This may mean that in relationships in which one partner has BPD, there can be conflict over sexual expectations and behaviors. The BPD partner may criticize or belittle a non-BPD partner who has little sexual experience, leading to arguments over sex. They also may be changeable in terms of their sexual wants and needs, leading to miscommunication and confusion.

Margaret and Ken

Ken was at his limit with Margaret. "Hot and cold" was how he described his wife to friends and family. Margaret could be the most loyal, loving woman one day and curse at Ken like a Marine sergeant the next. Her behavior in the bedroom was equally confusing. Margaret would aggressively initiate sex at times and seem insatiable. When Ken initiated in a similar manner, Margaret would push him away and accuse him of "exploiting" her. At times like that, Ken would become upset and withdrawn, which led to further accusations that he did not understand or love her.

After one particularly difficult bedroom episode in which Margaret accused Ken of being "like all men, a sex pig," Ken got up and left the house. When he returned, he found Margaret sobbing in the bathroom, blood running from little cuts she had made all along her wrist with a razor. Alarmed, Ken took Margaret to the nearest emergency room. Margaret was assessed to see if she was suicidal, which she denied, saying that she was just incredibly frustrated and angry with Ken. After further assessment, the psychiatrist told Margaret that he suspected she had BPD. After educating her, he prescribed an antidepressant and referred Margaret to a day treatment program. Although Ken was afraid Margaret would get angry at the psychiatrist, she was instead relieved to have a diagnosis and know there was hope of getting well. It would be a long road, but Ken hoped Margaret could find peace within herself and their marital problems could at last be resolved.

BPD is a challenge to treat. Couples must work to accept one another as individuals, communicate accurately, respond to one another without being overly reactive, effectively resolve problems, and maintain emotional closeness while preserving a solid sense of self. Couples' therapy may or may not help the couple achieve better sexual intimacy. Couples may be able to find a sex therapist who feels qualified to treat BPD couples, or they may need to attend couples' therapy, followed by sex therapy.

Narcissistic Personality Disorder

Narcissistic personality disorder (NPD) symptoms include having larger-than-life, grandiose ideas about being important, brilliant, and perfect, which results in an attitude of arrogance and intolerance. However, behind the mask of perfectionism, people with NPD are actually quite needy of approval and will look for admiration, adulation, and subservience to maintain an inflated sense of self. They lack empathy for and may be exploitive of others. The non-NPD partner can come to feel demeaned and demoralized by their NPD partner. They also may serve as a scapegoat for all of the failings of the relationship, including sexual problems, to sustain their intimate relationship.

A person with NPD may use sex to validate how attractive or special they are. They may become hypersexual, or overly interested in sex, and have multiple sexual partners as a way to gratify their need for admiration. Although the non-NPD partner may feel that they are also special because they have been "chosen" by a "superior" partner, they may eventually come to realize that they are in the relationship solely at the pleasure of the NPD partner.

If sexual or relationship problems arise, the NPD partner may blame the non-NPD partner, even if they themselves are mostly to blame. For example, if a male NPD partner develops erectile dysfunction (ED), they may accuse their partner of being boring in bed instead of recognizing that they have been drinking more than usual and are physically and emotionally numb. Sex becomes a proving ground for self-worth rather than a way to create a loving connection to a partner.

Stephen and Rebecca

Rebecca found Stephen incredibly difficult to please. No matter what she did, it was not good enough for him. Still, Rebecca stayed in the relationship because Stephen was an incredibly gifted physician who worked long hours and made a substantial income. However, when he was home, he expected Rebecca to wait on him hand and foot. If Rebecca complained, Stephen would arrogantly remind her of just how much money he earned and how she could never live their lifestyle on her own. In the bedroom, it was also all about Stephen.

Often Stephen would lie back while he watched Rebecca undress so he could see the breasts he had paid for, then demand Rebecca give him oral sex. Sometimes he would delay ejaculation so he could have intercourse with Rebecca, but more often, he ejaculated into her mouth, leaving Rebecca without satisfaction. It was not until Rebecca showed up in a therapist's office complaining of "no desire" that she realized what a toll Stephen's demands had taken on her self-esteem and her sex drive.

Some authors write about two types of narcissism: somatic and cerebral. The somatic narcissist is caught up with appearances of all types, but especially their looks. It is important for them to have a constant supply of admiration for being beautiful or handsome. This type of narcissist is more likely to see sex as validation for being attractive and special. The cerebral narcissist is more interested in being admired for their intellectual gifts. Cerebral narcissists are drawn to certain professions in which people will look up to them for their intelligence (e.g., minister, college professor, or physician). Because sex has little to do with intelligence, they may not be interested in sex at all. They also may not have much empathy for their partner's need for affection and sex.

Histrionic Personality Disorder

A histrionic personality disorder (HPD) is marked by a craving to be the constant center of attention, usually acquired through theatrical behavior and appearance. When they find themselves out of the spotlight, they may become even more flighty and dramatic to attract attention to themselves. Behind the theatrical mask, the person with HPD generally has low self-esteem. They tend to be sensitive and easily hurt by others. Their emotions are frequently shallow or seem forced or faked. Combined with a volatile personality, it can be difficult to maintain a relationship with an HPD partner.

Although there are men with HPD, most people with HPD are women who will use their appearance and sexuality to gain attention and possibly to manipulate others into meeting their needs. They may go so far as to sexualize a nonsexual relationship to gain needed attention. In other words, they may not want sex but rather to feed their need to be noticed and cared for. An HPD partner may display dramatic behavior if they feel rejected or hurt. Emotions are exaggerated and childlike. This dramatic behavior can be difficult for an intimate partner to cope with.

Julie and Ike

Ike was attracted to Julie like a moth to a flame. Julie wore very revealing clothing and had an impeccable hairstyle and a 150-watt smile. Ike was so blinded to Julie's light that he overlooked how flirtatious she was whenever they attended a party and assumed that she would stop once they married. It not only did not stop, it intensified, and Ike caught Julie in an extramarital affair that she called "nothing." But when

Ike caught her in a second affair, Julie blamed Ike, claiming that if he just given her more attention, she never would have needed to look elsewhere.

Antisocial Personality Disorder

It is very difficult for anyone to form a true relationship with a person who has antisocial personality disorder (ASPD). Also known by the term "sociopath," the person with APSD has usually developed a charming and socially capable façade behind which is a cold, uncaring self that can readily exploit others. Their charming exterior exists to help them deceive others. People with ASPD have very little emotion; if they form a relationship, its purpose is usually to exploit someone. Individuals who end up in the criminal system generally have some level of ASPD.

The person with ASPD who is interested in sex is generally promiscuous and will engage in infidelity and criminal sexual behavior such as sexual assault, rape, or pedophilia. The prognosis for treating an ASPD is very guarded. Although someone may be attracted to the idea of changing someone with ASPD through love and attention, people with ASPD rarely change; for that reason, it is advisable to avoid a relationship with a person with ASPD altogether unless they have undergone and continue intensive treatment.

CLUSTER C: ANXIOUS OR FEARFUL PDs

Obsessive-Compulsive Personality Disorder

Obsessive-compulsive personality disorder (OCPD) has some similarities to obsessive-compulsive disorder (OCD), but they are two distinct psychiatric illnesses. In OCD, the person feels compelled to perform rituals to feel relief from anxiety, but the relief is short-lived and the rituals must be performed repeatedly. OCPD is characterized by a preoccupation with rules and order. People with OCPD tend to be highly organized, demanding, and inflexible; they think in black and white, especially when it comes to moral values. They tend to be perfectionists, setting a high bar for themselves as well as everyone else. When others do not meet their standards, they may find themselves the object of anger and even rage. When they do not meet their own or somebody else's standards, whether real or imaginary, they can feel guilt and shame.

OCPD can interfere with enjoyment of many of life's pleasures, including sex. Men with OCPD can find themselves caught up with performance anxiety and ED. Because they tend to be highly anxious and demanding, they may also suffer with premature ejaculation. Men with OCPD can be easily distracted by anything that does not fit perfectly with the context of sex (e.g., squeaking bedsprings or a barking dog), which causes them to lose focus; this sometimes also leads to delayed ejaculation.

For women, performance anxiety and perfectionism can interfere with the ability to have orgasm. Many women who do not have orgasm also lose interest in sex. Women who have OCPD, perhaps more so than men who are less socialized around issues of cleanliness and hygiene, find such aspects of sex as smells and texture (pubic hair, beard) uncomfortable and even disgusting. They also may equate such things with germs and possible disease.

Patricia and Barry

If Patricia and Barry permitted their lovemaking to be filmed by a secret camera, anyone watching the playback would be puzzled. Before "commencing to have intercourse" (Patricia's words), the couple carefully brushed and flossed their teeth, showered separately, then appeared in clean nightclothes, all seemingly orchestrated by Patricia. Barry checked the thermostat while Patricia placed a tube of lubricant and a box of moistened personal wipes on the nightstand.

The couple then got under the covers together, where they felt one another's bodies over their pajamas. In a clinical manner, Barry stopped to apply lubricant to Patricia and then entered her in the missionary position. After a minute or two he stopped, apparently having had an orgasm. As he rolled onto his back, Patricia removed two wipes from the container, one for Barry and one for herself. Intercourse had ended. If Barry enjoyed himself, he did not say, but he had learned that this was the best sex he could expect from his wife of 20 years.

Partners of people with OCPD often find themselves at the receiving end of disappointment, frustration, and guilt if they do not live up to expectations. It can be difficult to maintain loving, intimate feelings with someone who seems to be judging one's actions most of the time. Sometimes, people who are drawn to those with OCPD have an issue themselves (e.g., attention deficit disorder [ADD] or a learning disability) and benefit from having a partner who is orderly and organized. Although this arrangement may work temporarily, the person with OCPD may become resentful and upset that their partner cannot conform to their standards.

Avoidant Personality Disorder

A person with avoidant personality disorder (AvPD) experiences intense social anxiety throughout their life. Sensitive to the possibility of rejection and feeling inadequate and inferior to others, they tend to avoid social situations. They often hold jobs in which they have little interpersonal contact with others, but beyond their incredible shyness, they usually do not appear as odd. Also, despite fear of social rejection, they have a strong wish for social relationships. However, their shyness may cause them to become withdrawn, aloof, or reclusive, making relationships very difficult.

People with an AvPD may enter into a romantic relationship, but achieving real intimacy may be difficult because of deep-rooted feelings of shame. This sense of shame may also extend to sexual behaviors, causing the partner with AvPD to be sexually inhibited. If male, they may struggle with ED and/or premature ejaculation. If female, they may have trouble achieving orgasm. It would not be unusual for a person with AvPD to develop an aversion to sex altogether because of the demand for openness and vulnerability. The anxiety experienced by a partner with AvPD may be just too great for sex to be pleasurable.

In addition to sexual difficulties, the non-AvPD partner suffers the same ups and downs that the AvPD partner experiences in terms of self-worth. One day, everything may seem fine; the next, the AvPD partner is certain that they are not worthy of love, which causes unhappiness and strife in the relationship.

Ned

Ned had great difficulty meeting women, especially after he graduated from college and was on his own. He tried Internet dating but found the experience of constantly meeting different women such a strain that he stopped after a couple of months. In addition, he was hiding a secret: He had difficulty waiting until penetration to ejaculate. Ned felt such shame about his sexual problems that he decided it was better to be single than to feel shame ever again.

Dependent Personality Disorder

Dependent personality disorder (DPD) is characterized by extreme neediness. Appearing childlike and frail, individuals with DPD want to be taken care of and will rely on others to make decisions for them. They have a fear of rejection and may become suicidal if a relationship goes sour or ends. They need a lot of reassurance and advice. They also tend to be sensitive to criticism or feedback.

Like the person with AvPD, the person with DPD is excessively anxious. But unlike the partner with AvPD, they are demonstrative about their neediness. In a romantic relationship, their partner may complain of feeling "smothered." A person with DPD may have sex with a partner to keep them interested enough that they will not be abandoned.

CLUSTER A: ODD AND ECCENTRIC PDs

People with Cluster A disorders are characterized by odd, eccentric behavior. A person with a paranoid personality generally has a great distrust of people.

They have difficulty getting along with others and tend to hold long grudges. Those with schizoid personality are emotionally detached from others, have poor social skills, and have little interest in having sexual experiences with another person. They are best characterized as "loners." An schizotypal personality presents as being odd or eccentric. They have uncommon beliefs, such as thinking that they are clairvoyant. They tend to be paranoid and socially anxious, emotionally constricted, and to have few, if any, social connections.

As you might gather, people with Cluster A disorders rarely enter into long-term romantic relationships. Even when presented with an opportunity to have sexual experiences, they may find them confusing and shy away. In my clinical experience, men with schizoid or schizotypal personality disorder will sometimes present in therapy for help with ED or premature ejaculation. Because they do not readily make a relationship with anyone, they tend to be poor candidates for therapy and, unfortunately, drop out prematurely. Since being male is a risk factor for schizotypal personality disorder, women with this problem very rarely appear in my office.

SEXUAL SOLUTIONS WHEN THE PROBLEM IS A PD

A common problem when one partner has a PD is that they may believe it is all right to behave one way outside of the bedroom and another way inside of the bedroom. An NPD partner may be demanding and difficult by day and then expect their partner to feel amorous by night because they themselves have not been troubled by their own behavior. Or, a DP partner who is needy and clinging and wants to make love to have proof of a partner's affection may find themselves rejected or made love to by a begrudging partner. Pairs in which one (or sometimes both) partner has BPD may find that they have worn each other out emotionally so that there is no energy left for sex. The partner married to someone diagnosed with OCPD may be annoyed by meticulous or stingy behavior, or the OCPD partner may withhold sexual pleasure as a punishment for the non-OCPD partner who has not complied with their wishes.

PDs may never disappear entirely, but they can be better managed. Sometimes the promise of a better sexual relationship can be highly motivating for couples affected by PD. Because PD can be thought of as a disorder of interpersonal relating, its treatment has the potential to substantially improve an intimate relationship.

Communication

Communication is always one of the keys to good sex, but it is critical when one or both members of a couple have a PD. Communication can be verbal as well as nonverbal; actions often do speak louder than words. For example, an NPD partner may become so involved in fantasies about admiring conquests, or an OCPD partner so distracted by the sound of squeaking bedsprings, that the non-PD partner feels frustrated or even abandoned. Being able to gently point out these problems without attacking a partner to maintain empathy and an open dialogue requires assertiveness and patience. Cultivating both qualities will create an atmosphere in which couples can work together to ensure that both partners' needs are met during lovemaking.

Stress

Stress can deflate almost anyone's sex life, but when one or both partners have a PD, the effects can be exacerbated because the pressures of life only increase the prominence and rigidity of maladaptive responses. Thus, managing stress is imperative not only for the couple's well being in the bedroom, but also in all kinds of relationship situations. Oddly, the PD partner may be resistant to stress management because their reactions feel "right" to them, although they ultimately undermine contentment. In addition, stress management is difficult in the beginning, but it does become more second nature if practiced consistently.

Attention to breathing and mindfulness are good stress management tools that have been addressed elsewhere in this volume, but time management and activity scheduling are also beneficial. Both partners can look at their schedules to see if there are tasks that can be eliminated, modified, or delegated to others. Schedules can also be changed so that there is time for such relaxing activities as listening to music or pursuing a hobby. Many couples also find that scheduling sex as a pleasurable activity, just as one might schedule a movie night, removes pressure and decreases anxiety over issues around initiation, rejection, and performance.

Decreasing interpersonal stress can also make intimacy more attainable. Improving listening skills, using assertive communication (e.g., making "I" statements), managing anger, and setting time aside to devote to problem-solving can all be learned and practiced in and out of the bedroom. Often, people with PD believe that their day-to-day behaviors are separate from bedroom behaviors. In addition, non-PD partners may withhold their frustration or other negative emotions for fear of escalating tension. Thus, when it comes time for intimacy, there may not be enough emotional or sexual energy to create sexual desire. That is why squarely facing PD, working on communication, and managing stress are important ingredients if a couple affected by PD is to have a satisfying sexual relationship.

Sensuality and Pleasure

Everyone is different, even when it comes to a group of people with a similar PD. However, in my clinical sex therapy practice, probably the most common complaint of partners is a lack of sensual touch. If you think about a PD as being a complex defense system, then you can understand why. The defenses are very much like a type of armor that protects a person. Taking that armor off for intimate lovemaking is not easy, especially because sex is one of the human activities that makes us most vulnerable. Thus, people with PD may be somewhat mechanical and focused more on keeping themselves mentally and emotionally protected during sex than letting themselves go and having pure enjoyment.

The sensate focus activities described in appendix 1 will be especially helpful. Go slowly to build trust. The non-PD partner needs to have patience and understand that becoming a sensual person, one who is learning to connect with another human being in a whole new way, will take time. The non-PD partner may, if possible, verbalize what he or she experiences, such as, "It feels peaceful to be close to you." Even if the PD partner does not express such feelings, they may learn over time to recognize them and feel safe enough to experience and share them.

RESOURCES

Books

Antony, Martin M., and Richard P. Swinson. *When Perfect Isn't Good Enough: Strategies for Coping with Perfectionism.* Oakland, CA: New Harbinger Publications, 2009.

Brown, Nina W. *Loving the Self-Absorbed: How to Create a More Satisfying Relationship with a Narcissistic Partner.* Oakland, CA: New Harbinger Publications, 2003.

Friedel, Robert O. *Borderline Personality Disorder Demystified: An Essential Guide for Understanding and Living with BPD.* New York: Marlowe & Company, 2004.

Hotchkiss, Sandy, and James F. Masterson. *Why Is It Always About You? The Seven Deadly Sins of Narcissism.* New York: Free Press, 2003.

Kantor, Martin. *Understanding Paranoia: A Guide for Professionals, Families, and Sufferers.* Westport, CT: Praeger, 2004.

Kreisman, Jerold J., and Hal Strauss. *I Hate You, Don't Leave Me: Understanding the Borderline Personality.* New York: Avon Publishing, 1991.

Markway, Barbara G., and Gregory P. Markway. *Painfully Shy: How to Overcome Social Anxiety and Reclaim Your Life.* New York: St. Martin's Press, 2003.

Mason, Paul T., and Randi Kreger. *Stop Walking on Eggshells: Taking Your Life Back When Someone You Care About Has Borderline Personality Disorder.* Oakland, CA: New Harbinger Publications, 2010.

Rufus, Anneli. *Party of One: The Loner's Manifesto.* New York: Marlowe & Co., 2003.

Stout, Martha. *The Sociopath Next Door: The Ruthless Versus the Rest of Us.* New York: Broadway Books, 2005.

Online Resources

American Psychological Association: http://www.apa.org/topics/personality/index.aspx.

Borderline Personality Disorder: BPD Central: http://www.bpdcentral.com/index.php.

Chapter Nine

PROBLEMS GENERALLY DIAGNOSED IN CHILDHOOD

Attention deficit disorder (ADD), Asperger's syndrome (AS), and learning disabilities are very different psychological problems. However, they have in common that they are usually first diagnosed in childhood. They can be missed because their symptoms are sometimes difficult for parents or teachers to detect or understand. Forgetfulness is an example of a symptom of ADD. Although everyone can relate to forgetting, it is hard to understand how someone might constantly lose the things they need all of the time, such as keys, cell phone, eyeglasses, wallet, jacket, etc. It may seem as if the forgetful person should have the willpower to overcome these symptoms, but they do not, even in adulthood. Although many adults with these disorders learn to compensate over time, symptoms may persist, affecting many facets of life.

In this chapter, of course, the focus is on the impact of these problems on relationships and sexuality. The fact that these disorders can cause problems with sexual relationships may come as a surprise, in part because such issues are simply overlooked, even by most mental health professionals. Unfortunately, many people enter into romantic and sexual relationships without any knowledge of sexual effects, which can range from minor (as in the case of ADD, drifting attention during a romantic dinner) to profound (as in the case of AS, mechanical sex or sexual avoidance). It is no wonder then that many couples seeking help in my sex therapy practice have one or sometimes both partners diagnosed with one of these mental disorders.

ADD

According to the National Institutes of Health, approximately 3–5 percent of the population of the United States has ADD. The hallmark symptom of ADD is an inability to concentrate, but there are many others, including forgetfulness, impulsivity, lack of organization, and difficulty staying on task. If a person fidgets, has trouble sitting still, seems keyed up, and is easily bored, then they are diagnosed with ADD, hyperactive type (sometimes called ADHD). If they daydream and have trouble with concentration, they are diagnosed with ADD, inattentive type. Someone can also be diagnosed with mixed type if they have some of the symptoms of each type.

Many people believe that children outgrow ADD when they become adults. Although some people with ADD do cope better with symptoms as they mature, many do not. In fact, sometimes people are not diagnosed with ADD until they need to meet the demands of adulthood, such as concentrating or being organized at work or behaving appropriately in intimate relationships. For example, they may have trouble paying bills on time or keeping on task, forget to purchase gifts and cards, speak impulsively to their partner, and so forth.

ADULT ADD MYTHS AND FACTS

Myth: People with ADD lack willpower. If they are able to focus on what interests them, then they could focus on other things if they wanted to.

Fact: Problems associated with ADD, such as forgetfulness or losing track of time, are not due to lack of willpower but to chemical problems with management systems in the brain.

Myth: If forgetfulness, daydreaming, and getting off track are symptoms of ADD, then everyone has it.

Fact: It is true that lots of people will experience some of the symptoms of ADD. It is the severity and the chronic nature of the symptoms that warrant a diagnosis.

Myth: You can only have ADD if it was diagnosed when you were a child.

Fact: ADD sometimes goes unrecognized in children. Some children also adapt or learn to cope with the symptoms of ADD, but when their lives as adults become more complex, they are expected to be more independent, or their symptoms cause a partner distress, they run into difficulties that may lead to a diagnosis.

Because ADD affects the ability to cope with everyday adult problems, its symptoms may create tension and negativity between partners. There are some typical patterns found in couples in which one partner has ADD that contribute to difficulties. One pattern occurs when an ADD partner who lacks organization and the ability to follow through with tasks will mate with an organized, parent-like partner. Although the non-ADD partner may initially find the ADD partner's live-in-the-moment approach refreshing, over time, the partner may find their impulsivity or inattentiveness annoying— after all, they signed on to be a partner, not a parent.

In another common pattern, the ADD partner becomes oppositional or argumentative as a way of seeking stimulation from the non-ADD partner. The ADD partner may also give feedback or ask questions in a blunt manner or tone, causing the non-ADD partner to react negatively. Partners also can unwittingly enter into a pattern of bickering. These patterns of interaction can make it difficult to create an atmosphere of emotional intimacy, which in turn can interfere with the couple's sexual relationship.

Mari and Ben

Married for two years, Mari and Ben's relationship had become an exercise in frustration. Because Mari and Ben chose not to live together before marrying, Mari did not really know just how forgetful Ben could be. After Ben left for work one Saturday morning, she found the milk in the dish cupboard, a month's worth of unpaid bills stuffed into an envelope, and a wrapper with a half-eaten hamburger under the seat of the car. Her blood boiling, there was no question that she would confront him as soon as he got home. So much for making love on their date night!

For his part, Ben was confused about Mari. He did not seem to know how to make her happy. All he wanted was to please her, but no matter how he tried to get more organized, he could not seem to measure up. And he did such stupid things, too! Then there was the bedroom, where Ben tried hard to have control over his ejaculation. Everything just seemed so intense during sex. It was getting so bad that he was losing his confidence and, on occasion, his erections, giving Mari even more reason to be annoyed with him. He had recently started to wonder if his teachers had been right—that he had ADD; however, like his parents, Ben felt that Mari would think of an ADD diagnosis as an excuse for his behavior. In addition, he did not want to take medicine because he feared he could become addicted.

Sexual activity requires the ability to focus on inner experiences and to share a physical and emotional event with a partner. The person with ADD may have a mind that wanders easily, which makes it challenging to achieve any one of these tasks. Whereas a non-ADD partner may be able to simultaneously give and receive sensations, during lovemaking, the ADD partner might think about work, a movie they want to see, and the next snack they want to eat, thus losing the point of what they are doing in bed.

Partners with ADD also can be too impulsive or impatient to spend time with foreplay. They may want to rush in to intercourse, leaving the non-ADD partner feeling unappreciated as well as underaroused. The inability to concentrate can also lead to erectile dysfunction (ED) and delayed ejaculation in men and to an inability to have an orgasm in women. It can also leave the non-ADD partner feeling lonely because they sense that their partner is not fully present for sex.

Sometimes people with ADD behave in a way opposite to what is expected by concentrating very hard on an activity, engaging in what is called "hyperfocus." (People sometimes believe that the ability to hyperfocus "proves" that someone does not have ADD, when in fact it is a very characteristic symptom.) In terms of sexual behavior, a man with ADD might become very attuned to sexual sensations and develop premature ejaculation. Women may also come to orgasm more quickly than their partner and then lose interest in continuing with sex.

People with ADD commonly like to experience new things to stimulate their minds. They will want to change positions, change locations, and try new sex toys. They may look for more and more intensity in their sexual encounters. The need for novelty can make what seems like perfectly fine lovemaking to the non-ADD partner dull for the ADD partner. However, if the non-ADD partner is sexually adventurous, this can be advantageous. If not, the non-ADD partner may find the ADD partner overly demanding at best or distasteful at worst.

This desire for novelty, combined with impulsivity, can sometimes lead people with ADD to enter into sexual affairs or seek out Internet pornography. They can be susceptible to risky sexual behaviors, such as entering chat rooms and meeting strangers for sex. (This is one reason that a problem like "sexual addiction" must be carefully evaluated so that underlying causes such as ADD can be identified and treated.) Thus, ADD symptoms can cause people to behave in ways that undermine their most important intimate relationship.

Sexual Solutions When ADD Is the Diagnosis

Treatment

The first step is for both partners to acknowledge the diagnosis and accept that the symptoms are not mainly under the control of the ADD partner. If the ADD partner is, overall, caring toward the non-ADD partner, then when things happen like forgetting appointments or losing items, it cannot be seen as "passive aggressive" or as signs that the ADD partner does not care.

However, that does not mean that the ADD partner has little responsibility for what happens within a relationship. The ADD partner may need to accept that to function optimally in a relationship, he or she will need to take medication. Although many people balk at the idea of medicine, most people with ADD appreciate its positive effect if they give it a try. They also need to learn tools and techniques to help shore up weaknesses like forgetfulness or difficulty keeping track of things.

The non-ADD partner needs to understand that for the relationship to run smoothly, he or she may need to supply their strengths around organization, memory, and follow-through and do so without resentment or belittling the ADD partner. As long as the ADD partner is taking medication and making a genuine effort to improve, the non-ADD partner has good reason to take on certain duties without feeling taken advantage of.

ADD and the Need for More Stimulation

The boredom that some people with ADD experience in daily life can also show up in a couple's sex life. The non-ADD partner can avoid being offended, knowing that this is just a symptom of ADD and not a personal criticism. Adding "spice" does not mean doing things that make one partner uncomfortable; the ADD partner should not use boredom as an excuse to coerce the non-ADD partner.

Experiment first with things that are easy to change: The room in which you make love, the color of the sheets, your undergarments, the lighting, music, etc. Consider changing positions, the order in which you please one another sexually, or looking at books of erotic photographs. Try sharing fantasies; however, make sure that you understand what your partner can tolerate. For example, some people are open to hearing about their partner's desire to be sexual with someone else; others are not. If you agree, then you can try acting out some fantasies together.

Facilitating Pleasure and Orgasm

People with ADD have a tendency to rush through things, even sex. They also may experience heightened sensitivity to touch, noise, and other sensations, making it difficult to enjoy foreplay. Sensate focus activities, as outlined in appendix 1, can help the ADD partner learn how to slow down and enjoy the sensation of touch. During sensate focus, partners can experiment by touching the body with textures like velvet or terry cloth or using lotion or talcum powder. Speed of touch may also help; the ADD partner may prefer a brisk rub or massage to a slow, sensual touch.

If it can be tolerated, couples may find eye-gazing and deep breathing to be pleasurable, slowing down action and creating a sense of emotional intimacy. Such an activity can also bring more mindfulness to sexual activity. Mindfulness is the act of staying present for what is happening in the moment, gently bringing the mind back to reality if it wanders. Paying close attention to sensations in itself can increase mindfulness. However, sometimes people with ADD find this type of exercise very difficult. If so, one partner can "narrate" what is happening as they make love. Partners also can switch being narrator and listener to increase attentiveness.

Of course, medication can also increase focus. You can talk with your prescribing physician about timing your dose, for example, on the weekends when you plan to be sexually active. There are also shorter-acting medications that can be taken when your primary medication has worn off, although care may need to be taken not to use them too close to bedtime. Also, it is not uncommon for people with ADD to have overlapping diagnoses of generalized anxiety disorder, major depression, or obsessive-compulsive disorder for which they may take antidepressants. Choosing an appropriate antidepressant or avoiding its use, if possible, by learning tools in cognitive therapy is important to maintaining good sexual function.

AS

The primary symptom of AS occurs when a person has great difficulty being conventionally social. AS is usually diagnosed in childhood, but it was only recognized as a mental disorder in 1994, so many adults have also recently been diagnosed with the syndrome. People with AS exhibit most of the following behaviors:

- Socially awkward, may have difficulty making or keeping friends
- Preoccupation with a certain subject
- Difficulty reading social cues, facial expressions, or body language
- Difficulty holding a conventional give-and-take conversation
- Finding emotions confusing or annoying
- Unaware of others' feelings; lacking in empathy and difficulty sharing in the emotional experiences of others
- Stilted manner of speaking
- May not enjoy physical closeness (e.g., holding hands)
- Honesty to the point of being tactless or brutal because of lack of empathy

As you might guess from these traits, an intimate relationship with a person with AS can be challenging for both parties. But people with AS do marry, sometimes quite happily.

Although people with AS differ from the "norm," they generally are clever and unique. (However, it is a myth that all people with AS are "geniuses"; IQ can fall along the full spectrum, from low to high.) In fact, they are often clever enough that they can learn how to "fake normal" by observing and parroting others, thus escaping detection, as well as hiding the psychological pain of not fitting in.

Roger and Ana
Ana was 33 years old and had just recovered from breaking up an eight-year relationship when she met Roger. Roger was everything her previous boyfriend had

not been: dependable, calm, predictable, and frugal. For his part, Roger found Ana's Latina facial features very appealing; her dark eyes reminded him of a beagle his family owned when he was small, a fact that Ana found charming. Because Roger often worked nights and weekends at a software company, the couple did not date that often. For Ana, this seemed fine because she was involved in her own career in finance. After the break-up of her long-term relationship, she was not especially interested in being sexual with someone from whom she did not have a commitment.

But once they got married, Ana discovered that Roger was not a very sensual lover. He complained about the smell of her saliva and noticed if she had a hangnail when she touched him. When they had intercourse, Roger buried his face in a pillow instead of making eye contact with her, and afterward he would jump up to shower by himself. Ana began to scold him, telling him that he was making her feel gross. Roger's response was to stop having sex with her altogether, staying on the computer and refusing to speak to her if he was especially angry. Frustrated to the point of considering divorce, Ana made an appointment with a therapist for herself and Roger. After a few meetings, the therapist told the couple that he thought Roger had AS.

Roger was not so much in shock as in denial. He did not believe that there was anything wrong with his lack of affection or his emotionally distant way of relating to Ana. He did not agree with the therapist that he thought of sex in ways that were overly mechanical. However, the pieces fell into place for Ana. Now she had a decision to make: accept Roger for the good qualities he had, seek sexual companionship outside of her marriage, or divorce.

If being married to a partner with AS is challenging, why would someone marry such a person? In his book *The Complete Guide to Asperger's Syndrome*, Attwood describes that people with AS may appear as socially immature, a quality that may attract a partner who has a parental quality. The non-AS partner may believe that through proper nurturing and interaction, the AS partner may gain insight and reciprocity. Also, the AS partner may not have had many relationships; thus, they have less "baggage" than other prospective partners, which may seem refreshing. They are also less interested in the physicality of their partner, which the non-AS partner may appreciate. People with AS generally have dedicated career interests; they seem to be good prospects in terms of earnings and stability. Finally, a person with AS with the ability to "fake normal" can act like someone who knows all about romantic involvement, saying and doing the right things. However, the person with AS may eventually tire of the ruse, or the non-AS partner may emerge out of denial, which can threaten the integrity of the relationship.

SEEKING AN AS DIAGNOSIS

There is no test for AS. A psychologist or other mental health professional who has an understanding of the disorder can make the diagnosis. People who are diagnosed as adults react differently. For some, the diagnosis is a relief. It helps them understand themselves better. As they and their family members learn about AS, pieces of the puzzle begin to fall into place. They may also feel less isolated knowing that there are others like them. The diagnosis also becomes a road map to making improvements, such as functioning better in social relationships and being a better romantic partner.

Other people may find the AS diagnosis to be distressing. They may dislike being labeled or feel embarrassed by having a known disorder. They may go into denial that there is anything wrong. They may not "believe in" AS. One thing is certain: You cannot force someone into accepting an AS diagnosis. If you have a partner who does not believe or denies an AS diagnosis, then you will need to do all you can to educate yourself and understand how to interact with him or her.

People with AS tend to view things in superficial, concrete ways. For example, they may state that they are attracted to their partner because of their hair color. When it comes to sex, they focus on the mechanics of the act rather than on emotions. They may seem withdrawn or absent rather than loving. Because making sex pleasurable requires attention to such nonverbal cues as facial expression or body language, the partner with AS may not be able to gauge what is and is not pleasurable for their non-AS partner.

Another problem is that many people with AS are uncomfortable with certain sensations. They may dislike the smell of their partner or the feel of their hair rubbing against them. Sensual experiences may elude them altogether. The non-AS partner may complain that their AS partner is "cold" in bed. They may also resent that if sex is going to happen, it is up to them to initiate and to take charge of the couple's sexual script; that is, the way the encounter plays out between the sheets.

Trying to have a romantic relationship with an AS partner can lead to low self-esteem for the non-AS partner. A partner wishing for a deep connection may be disappointed, even to the point of feeling lonely and depressed. The AS partner may realize that they have failed to act appropriately, or that they will not be able to meet the non-AS partner's expectations, and start to withdraw in the bedroom.

Sexual Solutions When AS Is the Diagnosis

Accurate Diagnosis

If you are reading this section of the chapter because you are wondering if your partner has AS, then it is best to see a mental health professional for an assessment. Being "nerdy" simply is not enough to warrant the diagnosis; many highly intelligent and unconventional people are able to read social cues and connect well with others. If a diagnosis is made, be aware that the person with AS may have difficulty accepting it because they may truly believe they are perfectly fine as is. You may also have trouble accepting and understanding a diagnosis, because now your partner's bothersome behaviors are not just a matter of will and can not be changed given the right motivation. Overall, a diagnosis may help both partners to accept certain behaviors and to figure out how to cope with or work around those behaviors that interfere with the relationship.

Because living with and loving someone with AS can be very complex, most authors advocate counseling with a psychologist or psychotherapist who has experience working with couples affected by AS. Even if the AS partner is uninterested in counseling, the non-AS partner may want insight into ways in which they can better cope with having a partner with AS. If you do seek counseling and sex is part of the problem, be sure to ask the therapist if they are comfortable working with sexual issues.

Pragmatic Approaches to Sex

If the relationship in which a partner has AS is to survive, then the non-AS partner has to develop realistic expectations about sex. Often the AS partner wants to please their dissatisfied non-AS partner but is unsure of how to proceed. It is best if the dissatisfied partner can put aside hurt or angry feelings and realize that the person with AS is not willfully withholding sexual pleasure. They need to help the AS partner become a better sexual partner, which is done by telling the partner with AS explicitly how to proceed with sex. Letting the AS person know the "order" in which you would like things to occur can also be helpful; that is, tell the person that you would like to start off with a hug, and then proceed to some kissing, followed by undressing, etc.

Scheduling sex is also a good idea. It minimizes anxiety and helps the AS person who typically has difficulty with spontaneity and transitions to a new activity. Although this approach may seem to be exactly what the non-AS partner seeks to avoid—mechanical sex—it may be better to have some sexual satisfaction than none at all, and it may diminish the need to consider such alternatives as having an affair or divorcing.

Decreasing Sensitivity to Sexual Sensations

The non-AS partner can be understanding and supportive of the AS partner's needs when it comes to sensual activities. If the AS partner is more willing to make love when the non-AS partner is wearing lip balm or wears a silky garment to bed, then the request should be seriously considered. The AS partner and non-AS partner can consider switching off how they will have sex. In marriages in which a partner has AS, other aspects of sex can also be negotiated. For example, if the AS partner has trouble initiating, or the non-AS partner finds the approach too blunt or unromantic, they can come up with a subtler signal that the AS partner is in the mood for sex.

LEARNING DISABILITIES

Approximately 2 percent of the U.S. adult population has an identifiable learning disability. Learning disabilities decrease a person's abilities to understand, remember, or express information or to learn new skills, which affects their intellectual and social development throughout life. People with learning disabilities may have difficulties with spoken and written language, coordination, attention, or self-control. Often, learning disabilities coexist with other conditions, including physical impairments, sensory impairments, or behavioral disorders.

The discussion of learning disabilities and sexuality will be limited to people whose intelligence is in the normal range and above. There is very little research on the impact of learning disabilities on marital and sexual relationships. However, in my clinical practice, I have worked with several couples whose challenges with intimacy are related to one partner's learning disability, so I felt it was important to include learning disability in this chapter.

Learning disabilities generally manifest in the following ways:

- Differences in processing language and speech
- Reading difficulties
- Math difficulties
- Fine motor skills, such as used when holding tools or utensils
- Large motor skills that affect balance and coordination
- Writing difficulties

People with learning disabilities may also have problems with memory and concentration, including symptoms of ADD. Sadly, people with learning disabilities are often misunderstood as being unintelligent, when the fact is that learning disabilities can affect people with a broad range of IQs. In addition, as children and teens, they usually face teasing and bullying because of their difference, which can lead to low self-esteem and depression.

Like couples affected by ADD, couples affected by learning disabilities often consist of one learning-disability partner and one nonlearning-disability partner who acts in a caregiving role. In some cases, this works out well. The nonlearning-disability partner may have natural patience and a tendency toward caregiving, or have a real understanding of the limitations and the strengths of the learning-disability partner. The learning-disability partner will also understand his or her strengths and limitations, taking responsibility to do what they can to take care of themselves. However, some couples are not as well matched.

Sheila and Terrence

Sheila had been diagnosed with a math learning disability in elementary school. Her concerned and well-meaning parents did everything they could to help Sheila, ferrying her to specialists, after-school programs, and tutors so that she could finish high school. What her parents did not prepare her for was falling in love and being sexually active with Terrence, an ex-Marine who wanted to marry and care for Sheila. Although her parents felt Sheila was not ready for marriage, Sheila was an adult, and they gave the couple a wedding.

Initially, Terrence busied himself setting up their apartment and making sure things were structured for efficiency. But Terrence soon became frustrated with Sheila, who had a hard time following Terrence's schedule and instructions. She was unable to help him out with paying bills or grocery shopping. She depended on Terrence to drive her to all of her appointments. Soon Terrence could not hold back his resentment and annoyance and began to put Sheila down. Sheila's self-esteem was not much to begin with, so she had trouble standing up for herself. As Terrence grew more distressed, he withdrew sexually, leaving Sheila feeling rejected and even more guilty and ashamed. By the time they made it to marriage counseling, Terrence had had an affair and they were on the verge of divorcing.

Men and women with learning disabilities often lag in their emotional and social development. Although someone with learning disabilities may have a mature appearance, adequate verbal skills, and good manners, they may not entirely understand all of the negotiations that go into maintaining a complex social relationship. At the same time, they can be eager to please; along with being socially naïve, they are sometimes targets for partners who are exploitive, violent, abusive, or otherwise inappropriate. For the same reason, people with learning disabilities are sometimes victims of sexual and other abuse as children; the more profound the learning disability, the more likely they are to have been abused. Because their needs can put a strain on family resources, they can also be scapegoats for many problems, furthering wearing on self-esteem.

Like the non-ADD partner, the nonlearning-disability partner needs to educate him- or herself about the particular type of learning disability their partner has. They will need to discuss their role in the learning-disability partner's life, as well as what they both expect the learning-disability partner's responsibilities will be. Neither partner should take lightly the effect of learning disabilities on their relationship but should work out a division of labor to avoid misunderstandings and resentment.

Sexual Solutions When the Problem Is a Learning Disability

People with learning disabilities may not have a sexual dysfunction per se, but relationship problems may affect physical and emotional intimacy. However, communication is difficult for most every couple when it comes to sex. If the learning-disabled partner has a language-processing problem, then communication challenges can be magnified. Also, people with learning disabilities are often sensitive to feedback because they may not understand it right away or they may have built up defensiveness from years of feeling or being criticized. Because learning disabilities vary widely, it is helpful to understand how a learning-disability partner best processes information and to calmly and simply discuss any sexual difficulties.

Sexual Knowledge

Oftentimes, parents of offspring with learning disabilities fail to educate them about sex because they see their children as being too naïve or because they are overly protective. Thus, some adults with learning disabilities reach adulthood without much sexual knowledge. Sexual knowledge includes not just the techniques of lovemaking, but also how the body works; defining one's own sexual boundaries; communicating one's sexual wants and needs; understanding the responsibilities inherent in becoming a sexual partner (e.g., good communication, using birth control, and practicing safe sex); and knowing that sex should be a give-and-take, pleasurable activity that does not include coercion or abuse.

Partners should work together to ensure that they both have similar sexual knowledge. For example, both partners should understand how pregnancy occurs and how to prevent unwanted pregnancy through birth control; assumptions should not be made. Both partners also need to acknowledge that they each have the right to say no to any type of sexual activity or to engaging in any activity at all. Both partners can learn about sexual pleasure if they access materials (e.g., *The Guide to Getting It On* by Paul Joannides or http:// www.sexualhealth.com).

Couples in which one partner has a learning disability may also want to ensure that they have an understanding nurse or physician on their team who they can go to with such sexual concerns as ED or inability to have orgasm. The learning-disability partner may need someone to show them sexual anatomy on a model or in a book or to explain how anxiety or lack of attention can interfere with sexual function (e.g., having an erection or relaxing enough to have an orgasm).

RESOURCES

Attention Deficit Disorder

Books

Halverstadt, Jonathan. *A.D.D. & Romance*. Lanham, MD: Taylor Trade Publishing, 1998.
Pera, Gina. *Is It You, Me, or Adult A.D.D.? Stopping the Roller Coaster When Someone You Love Has Attention Deficit Disorder*. San Francisco: 1201 Alarm Press, 2008.

Online Resources

ADDittude Magazine: http://www.addittudemag.com.
Attention Deficit Disorder Association: http://www.adda.org.

Asperger's Syndrome

Books

Attwood, Tony. *A Complete Guide to Asperger's Syndrome.* Philadelphia: Jessica Kingsley Publishers, 2008.

Marshack, Kathy J. *Life with a Partner or Spouse with Asperger Syndrome: Going over the Edge? Practical Steps to Savings You and Your Relationship.* Shawnee Mission, KS: Autism Asperger Publishing, 2009.

Stanford, Ashley. *Asperger's Syndrome and Long-Term Relationships.* Philadelphia, PA: Jessica Kingsley Publishers, 2002.

Chapter Ten

SEVERE MENTAL ILLNESS

The topic of sexuality and severe mental illness has been addressed in articles and books that are generally aimed at managing the sexual behaviors of mentally ill adults in inpatient settings. This fact only adds to the mythology that people with schizophrenia and other disorders may act out inappropriately and are to be feared or, conversely, are asexual and have no sexual drive or interest at all. In fact, people with severe mental illness, if they are properly medicated and treated, do express needs, but mainly for affection and companionship. Although a discussion of the ethics of sexual behavior in inpatient settings is beyond the scope of this book, an exploration and understanding of the intimate needs of people with severe mental illness is essential.

SCHIZOPHRENIA

Schizophrenia is a group of severe brain disorders in which people have difficulty discerning reality and fantasy. There is usually a combination of hallucinations, delusions, and disorders of thought and behavior. The most common symptom is delusions, or beliefs that are not based in reality. Hallucinations involve seeing or hearing things that do not exist; hallucinations may also involve other symptoms. With a thought disorder, the person with schizophrenia may have difficulty organizing and expressing their thoughts. Behavior disorders can be expressed as bizarre behavior, childlike actions, or agitation. There can also be mood swings as well as other mental disorders, including substance abuse; past childhood emotional, physical, or sexual trauma; and phobias (fears).

Given all of these common symptoms, it may be difficult to understand why the sexuality of a person with schizophrenia needs to be addressed at all. For many people, including mental health professionals, the idea of a person who is psychotic or schizophrenic being sexual is off-putting. For example, many people with schizophrenia have symptoms that make them lethargic and appear to have no emotional feelings, suggesting that the person with schizophrenia has no need to be in an intimate relationship, either sexual or nonsexual. But a person who has a severe mental illness may be quite capable of having thoughts and feelings about the topics of love and sex. He or she may want someone to hang out with, to talk to, or to watch television with; someone to hug and kiss; and even someone with whom to enjoy intercourse. People who treat or live with someone with a psychotic disorder may fear that acknowledgment of the person's sexuality or the provision of sex education could result in promiscuity or sexual acting out. However, to withhold knowledge or to be judgmental is to dehumanize and desexualize another human being with real needs.

Molly and Trevor

Molly and Trevor met at an inpatient treatment center. They both were being treated for schizoaffective disorder, or schizophrenia with major depression. The couple discovered that they shared an interest in *Star Trek* and sat on the sofa in the community room talking about the characters for hours. Soon they began to hold hands. The staff took notice and warned them not to become sexual with one another. But Trevor wanted to take it further. He went to the director of the facility and asked why they were not allowed to have sex. The director, although sympathetic, explained that the facility did not want to be responsible if either person had a sexually transmitted disease or if a pregnancy occurred. Trevor and the director struck an agreement that he and Molly could be affectionate without being punished by staff.

Schizophrenia is rare, occurring in approximately 1 percent of the population. Its cause is unknown, although there are certain risk factors, including having a family history of schizophrenia, stressful life circumstances, and taking psychoactive drugs in adolescence and young adulthood. Schizophrenia is a chronic condition that is not curable but can be managed with antipsychotic medications and psychosocial therapy. A person with schizophrenia may need to be hospitalized, sometimes many times, if they are unable to care for themselves or become suicidal or homicidal.

The average age of onset for males is in the late teens or early twenties; for females, it generally appears in the late twenties, thirties, or even forties. For that reason, it is more likely that women may be in a long-term relationship or marriage when the illness first becomes problematic. The onset can be insidious; that is, it can take many years of slow deterioration before a diagnosis is made. Depression, brief psychotic disorder lasting less than a month, and schizotypal personality disorder are some of the illnesses that are mistakenly diagnosed before the person is given the diagnosis of schizophrenia.

For many reasons, the marriage rate is low and the divorce rate is high for people with schizophrenia. Marriage to and between people with severe mental illness is generally discouraged. Even Freud cautioned his male patients not to marry women that had "nervous trouble." In one study of 22 married couples with at least five years of psychiatric treatment, half of them had been advised not to marry by family members and mental health professionals.

One reason marriage is difficult is because the partner with schizophrenia may become dependent on the nonschizophrenic partner when they have a relapse of their illness. People with schizophrenia often have difficulty with day-to-day functioning, such as hygiene, feeding oneself, and conducting tasks both large and small. They may be noncompliant with taking medications, which can cause relapse and rehospitalization. Even when compliant with medication, approximately 47 percent of sufferers continue to have persistent psychotic symptoms, making recovery uncertain.

In her remarkable book, *The Center Cannot Hold: My Journey through Madness*, law professor Elyn R. Saks describes her lifelong struggle with depression and schizophrenia. Saks is married and she describes her husband as kind and patient. The couple is definitely sexual with each other. However, her husband does need to be vigilant to Saks' mental state and needs to call her psychiatrist or take her to the hospital for treatment. Saks' experiences are inspiring, but they are atypical. Saks seems to have excellent financial resources, an exceptionally brilliant mind, and good social skills that win her friends wherever she goes, even in the psychiatric ward. That is not to say that each person with schizophrenia needs to have similar resources to marry, but Saks' story can also be read as a cautionary tale, letting people know just what occurs when someone has schizophrenia and the kinds of support that may be required to sustain an intimate relationship. Each couple facing the challenge of schizophrenia will be unique.

PSYCHOSIS

Psychosis is diagnosed when a person loses contact with reality. The most common symptoms of psychosis are having false ideas about what is taking place or about one's identity (delusions). A person with psychosis may also hear or see things that others cannot (hallucinations). Various conditions can cause psychosis, including alcohol and other drugs during use and withdrawal, brain tumors, degenerative brain illnesses such as Parkinson's or Huntington's disease, Alzheimer's disease and dementia, and certain prescription drugs. Psychosis can also be part of several psychiatric disorders, including depression with psychotic features, bipolar disorder, personality disorder (e.g., schizotypal, schizoid, and borderline), and schizophrenia.

Most often, the cause of psychosis can be pinpointed, occasionally through laboratory tests and also through psychiatric evaluation. Psychosis is treated with antipsychotic medications, whether the problem is medical or psychiatric. Additional treatment will depend on the cause. For example, surgery may be required for a brain tumor, whereas rehabilitation will be required for alcoholism.

How sexuality is affected will also depend on the cause and its treatment as well as the couple's relationship before the psychotic episode occurred. In her book *Sex When You're Sick*, Anne Katz, RN, describes how couples can maintain a sexual relationship when faced with a chronic illness. Other chapters in Katz's book address sexuality and other mental illnesses.

DEMENTIA AND ALZHEIMER'S DISEASE

Dementia is a medical term that is used to describe the gradual loss of several mental functions, including memory impairment, difficulty with language, failure to recognize people and objects, decreased motor skills, and the inability to plan or think abstractly. The affected individual can also have difficult learning or retaining new information. Paranoia and other displays of inappropriate behavior are also possible.

Alzheimer's disease is one form of dementia. One of the primary differences between Alzheimer's disease and dementia is that it can occur earlier in life and can be diagnosed in people as young as 45, whereas dementia occurs in elderly people, usually over age 70. There are other diseases associated with dementia, including vascular diseases that affect the flow of blood to the brain, Huntington's disease, HIV-associated dementia, and Lewy Body dementia. All dementias are progressive, and there is no known cure.

Thinking about dementia and sexuality will be such a far stretch for many people that the topic rarely comes up, even in support groups and the offices of professionals who treat dementia and its related problems. In fact, the caregiving partner may have very strong emotions about the loss of his or her partner's ability to be sexual. Not only is the affected partner's memory impaired, but their motor skills may be awkward or difficult to coordinate. In addition, medications used to treat the symptoms of dementia may interfere with sexual desire and function.

Catherine and Frank

The diagnosis of Alzheimer's disease was devastating to Catherine and Frank. Catherine was 60 and Frank was 65; they had planned so well for retirement—a cruise to the Caribbean, a trip to Paris—but Catherine was having a hard time remembering how to navigate their home; there was no possible way she could manage to travel. As the shock of the diagnosis wore off, Frank noticed that he felt very uncomfortable approaching his wife for sex. He feared that asking his wife to make love would be taking advantage of her in some way. With no one to turn to, he finally expressed his frustration to the therapist he had begun seeing to help him cope with caregiving. The therapist reminded him that he and Catherine had a 20-year history of being sexual with one another. If Catherine consented to have sex, then there was nothing wrong with making love.

Later that week, Frank decided to play some music that he and Catherine had always enjoyed. Catherine surprised him by coming up to him and grabbing him to dance. Feeling Catherine's body aroused him, and Catherine noticed. Although they did not have intercourse, they did touch each other's genitals to orgasm. Frank was not certain that Catherine would remember their encounter, but he felt good that they had been sexual together and decided to enjoy whatever physical contact they had.

SEXUAL SOLUTIONS WHEN THE PROBLEM IS SEVERE MENTAL ILLNESS

Medications

Neuroleptic and antipsychotic drugs can have many sexual side effects, including loss of desire, decreased drive, poor sexual performance, premature ejaculation, erectile dysfunction, and delayed ejaculation and lack of orgasm. Other side effects (e.g., weight gain and sedation) can also interfere with sexual pleasure and function. In fact, sexual difficulties can be one reason that people stop their medications. It is therefore imperative that sufferers and their partners not ignore or give up on their sexual needs and address sexual side effects with the prescribing medical doctor.

Preventing Relapse, Building Intimacy

Couples who wish to stay together in the long term need to also work together to prevent relapse. Together, couples can track signs and symptoms on a daily basis to catch any deterioration in mood or functioning early, before the partner with severe mental illness goes into crisis. The nonaffected partner can track observations, whereas the affected partner can track experiences. It also helps the nonaffected partner to see the affected partner taking responsibility for his or her own mental health.

In addition to tracking symptoms, lifestyle habits can also promote mental health. Getting enough sleep, eating regular meals, and avoiding the use of alcohol, recreational drugs, and nonprescribed medications like painkillers can help both partners stay on an even track. Regular exercise and taking time for real relaxation such as yoga can also be of great benefit.

Affected partners can also take control of their environment as much as possible. In terms of interacting with other people, the affected partner can decide how many people are manageable at a time, and interact, as much as possible, only with those people with whom they have a positive experience. They can limit how much noise they are exposed to and even the types of movies they watch, avoiding those that can trigger unwanted emotional responses. It is also important to have tasks to do to avoid long stretches of unscheduled time, but not so much to do that it is overwhelming.

RESOURCES

Books

Saks, Elyn R. *The Center Cannot Hold: My Journey through Madness.* New York: Hyperion, 2007.

Torrey, E. Fuller. *Surviving Schizophrenia: A Manual for Families, Friends, and Patients.* New York: Collins, 2006.

Woolis, Rebecca. *When Someone You Love Has a Mental Illness: A Handbook for Family, Friends, and Caregivers.* New York: Jeremy P. Tarcher/Putnam, 2003.

Online Resources

National Institute of Mental Health: http://www.nimh.nih.gov/health/topics/schizophrenia/index.shtml.

WebMD: Schizophrenia: http://www.webmd.com/schizophrenia/guide/schizophrenia-support-resources.

Chapter Eleven

LOVE AND MENTAL ILLNESS: TIPS FOR PARTNERS

Being in a relationship with someone who has a psychological problem can be challenging. Mental illnesses are medical and psychological conditions that interfere with a person's thinking, feeling, mood, ability to relate to others, and daily functioning. Mental illnesses often impair a person's capacity for coping with life's demands, both large and small. Serious mental illnesses include major depression, schizophrenia, bipolar disorder, obsessive-compulsive disorder, panic disorder, post-traumatic stress disorder, and borderline personality disorder.

Mental illnesses do not occur because a person is weak, lacks character, or had faulty parenting. They cannot be willed away and should not be ignored. Many mental illnesses, if left untreated, can be fatal. Fortunately, appropriate and effective treatment can lessen the impact of mental illness on a person's life, which can help them function normally at work, at home, and in their relationships. The earlier the stage at which the illness is detected and treated, the more likely it is that recovery will happen more quickly and fully and the less the impact there will be on the person's well being. Most mental illnesses are not so much cured as they are managed through a combination of medication and psychotherapy. This chapter assumes that the partner or partners with mental illness are receiving appropriate treatment and are in remission or working toward remission of their condition.

DIFFERENT DEGREES OF MENTAL ILLNESS

Each type of disorder has a continuum from mild to severe. Mild, transient depression lasting less than six weeks is much different from severe major depression with suicidal ideation. Bulimia can range from purging with diuretics on Monday after a weekend of binge eating to bingeing and purging several times a day. If a person obsessively looks at their e-mail and bank balance, that is not disruptive; if a person cannot leave their house unless they check every outlet, appliance, window, and door, taking an hour or more to do so, then that can get in the way of the person's ability to function.

It is nearly impossible to be in a relationship with someone who has an uncontrolled severe mental illness. Individuals with severe mental illness will become consumed by their symptoms and even defend them. They may not have the insight to recognize that their thoughts and behaviors are irrational. They must have appropriate treatment to function appropriately in a relationship. It will not help to stay in denial when things are clearly wrong. A person who has an out-of-control disorder needs to be evaluated and treated.

GET GOOD ASSESSMENT AND TREATMENT

Make sure that you see the appropriate mental health professionals. When it comes to moderate to severe mental illness, you should seek the help of a psychiatrist and psychologist. A psychiatrist can make an assessment and prescribe medication. Sometimes a psychiatrist will make a referral to a psychologist, who can take more time to assess a person's illness. This is important because there are sometimes overlapping disorders. For example, a person with bipolar disorder can also have obsessive-compulsive disorder, or a person with post-traumatic stress disorder may also have attention deficit disorder. It is important to get an exact diagnosis to get appropriate treatment.

GRIEVE THE LOSS

In my experience, people have mixed reactions to being diagnosed with a mental disorder. Some are relieved to find out that there is a name and treatment, but others are in shock and need time to process that there is "something wrong with me." When it comes to couples, it is the partner who may have trouble hearing and accepting a diagnosis. It is normal to feel a little overwhelmed and sad to find out that you have a disorder that is not going to go away simply by wishing. Give yourselves time to become adjusted and to accept that there needs to be a "new normal."

BECOME KNOWLEDGEABLE

Learn all you can about the diagnosed mental disorder. You should be able to recognize symptoms and any potential triggers. You should also understand the various types of treatment available; different types of treatment may be appropriate at different times. For example, cognitive behavioral therapy (CBT) may be used soon after diagnosis to help decrease symptoms quickly, often along with medication. Once the person affected has control over their symptoms, couples' therapy may be helpful.

FIND SUPPORT

Unfortunately, many people neglect to get good social and emotional support because of the stigma of mental illness. However, such support can be very helpful to the partner with the illness and the non-ill partner. Support may come from mental health professionals, pastors, and rabbis and from such organizations as the National Alliance for the Mentally Ill (NAMI). When seeking support from friends and family members, you and your partner should be in agreement about which friends and family members you can count on for real support. People who provide ongoing support should also be educated about the illness.

COUPLES' COUNSELING

Couples' counseling when one partner has a mental disorder needs to include education for both partners. Whether the therapist is a psychologist with a doctorate or a master's-level therapist, he or she should be trained in couples' therapy and have good knowledge about the disorder that has been diagnosed. Do not assume that all therapists have the same level of training or interest. If one of you has a diagnosis with an eating disorder, then find a therapist who has specialized interest or training, if at all possible. Not all therapists are good at marketing their specialties, so it may be worthwhile to ask a therapist about his or her experience.

TAKE RESPONSIBILITY

The ill partner must take responsibility for the treatment and management of their disorders. They need to take medications as prescribed, go to therapy, recognize symptoms of relapse, be honest about the return of symptoms, and not use illness as an excuse to avoid doing things. If they experience the return of symptoms, they need to be honest and take steps to avoid a relapse or exacerbation of their illness. They also need to build a team of support for themselves, finding professionals and support groups to help them because their partner cannot do it all.

YOU CANNOT FIX YOUR PARTNER

No matter how hard you try, no matter how much you may want your partner to be well, you cannot fix him or her. Do not take it upon yourself to make your partner into a "fix-it" project. Find someone with the necessary education and skills to treat your partner.

FIND OTHER ACTIVITIES

The well partner can become overly caught up in the challenges of being the partner of someone with a mental illness. This is not only stressful for the well partner, but can also put a strain on the marital relationship. Find a hobby, develop your career, take a class, or learn to play a musical instrument. You need to lead your own life, too.

ANTICIPATE SETBACKS

Sometimes both partners assume that once someone has been diagnosed and treated that the illness has been "cured." There is no cure for mental illness. Even with appropriate management of symptoms, a person with mental illness may experience a setback. There is often no one to blame for such events. It is better to accept that symptoms may return. Understand the symptoms and know what to do if and when they do reappear.

ROUTINES

As much as possible, try to eliminate chaos from the home. Establish routines for sleeping and waking, meals, chores, shopping, laundry, etc. Having a regular, predictable rhythm can help all family members manage stress and keep the household calm.

ACCEPTING MAJOR CHANGE

Accept what the partner with a disorder cannot manage (e.g., paying bills, doing certain household chores, having overnight visits from friends or relatives, or keeping time commitments). If your partner cannot hold a full-time job, then accept that you may need to become a full-time provider. If your partner cannot tolerate socializing at gatherings such as large parties and weddings, accept that you may need to go alone or find someone else to accompany you.

Sometimes role changes are very tough on a relationship and can affect intimacy and sexuality more than anything else. We all have ideas about what a man or a woman "should" do in a marriage or partnership. Although it is natural to be a bit upset or put out when change first happens, it is important for your own and your partner's well being to accept change. Remember, both partners have feelings of loss about their roles. It can be critical to get outside support or therapy to manage feelings of anger and resentment to keep the relationship intact.

APPENDIX 1

SENSATE FOCUS ACTIVITIES

William Masters and Virginia E. Johnson were the originators of sex therapy, and this is their classic activity for couples. This series of activities is designed to do several things, including:

- Focus you on pleasure instead of performance; decrease anxiety
- Increase a sense of connection
- Establish or reestablish a good sex life

Here is the basic exercise. Variations follow. Please note that intercourse is off-limits until the later stages of the activity.

Sensate Focus I

- You will be taking turns sensually caressing, stroking, and feeling your partner's hands, arms, feet, and legs.
- Set aside 20 minutes, three times during the week.
- Select a setting in which you will have uninterrupted privacy. You can make the scene romantic with music, candles, etc.
- Agree to do this activity clothed or lightly clothed (e.g., shorts and tank top).
- You will split the 20-minute time into two 10-minute periods. One of you will be the receiver and one the giver of touch during each 10-minute period.
- You can use a coin to decide who will go first if you would like. You can also decide ahead of time how you want to plan or figure out who will initiate first.

- One of the reasons the word "focus" is in the title of this activity is that you are supposed to focus on your own sensations instead of your partner's responses (or what you think are your partner's responses). If what you are doing to your partner feels good to you, chances are very good it also feels good to your partner.
- Try to talk as little as possible during the exercise. You can give feedback later, perhaps the next morning or sometime before you repeat the activity. Refrain from giving feedback right after the activity, when your partner's defenses may be down. They may feel too vulnerable then to take in your suggestions, such as the fact that you need firmer touch.

Sensate Focus II

- Sensate Focus II includes exploration of the breasts and genitals.
- Follow the guidelines in Sensate Focus I regarding time, frequency, and tuning in to one's own sensations.
- Start the activity with general touching of the hands, arms, feet, and legs; do not move immediately to the breasts or genitals.
- You can do this activity nude or with light clothing, as you prefer.
- Try including a "hand-riding" technique. When it is your turn to be the receiver, place your hand on your partner's hand to gently guide them into understanding how much pressure, how fast or slow, or what particular areas you like to have caressed. Do not take control; just add a little input to what the giver is doing.

Sensate Focus III

- Same idea as Sensate Focus I and II, but now the touching is mutual.
- Shift your attention to your enjoyment of your partner's body.
- If you become highly aroused, take a little break and resume touching. The point is to enjoy the journey, not just the destination.

Sensate Focus IV and V

- Continue as in previous activity sessions.
- At some point, move to the female-on-top position without attempting insertion of the penis into the vagina.
- In this position, the woman can rub her clitoris, vulva, and vaginal opening against her partner's penis regardless of whether or not there is an erection.
- Eventually, the woman can insert the tip of the penis into the vagina if there is an erection. Go back to nongenital pleasuring if either partner becomes anxious.
- After doing this type of play a few times, you will most likely feel ready for intercourse. Keep the focus on your sensations and on non-demand pleasuring.

APPENDIX 2

MINDFULNESS AND SEXUAL PLEASURE

One thing that makes sex pleasurable is the ability to forget troubling thoughts, calm the body, and focus on your own body's sensations. You and your partner let the world fall away and enter into a trance of sorts in which the only thing that matters is the sensual experience that the two of you share. For many individuals and couples, this is a process that comes naturally. Partners are both relaxed, their stress has been managed and put away, and they have an idea or "script" in their minds about how lovemaking is about to happen.

For people with a mood, anxiety or other problem, relaxing and letting go may not occur so easily. They may have difficulty pushing unwanted thoughts or feelings away, including wondering about sexual performance or believing themselves to be sexually inadequate. Mindfulness, or being fully present in the moment, is one way to be able to experience sexual activity with a fresh and open mind.

But the best time to learn to be mindful probably is not when you are having sex. There may be too much going on, at first, for you to be able to touch your partner and focus on your own state of being. Not to worry: there are plenty of other ways to learn the lessons of mindfulness.

One way is through the act of eating. A classic mindful activity is to take an orange (or other fruit, if you prefer) in your hands. As you hold the orange, take a few deep, calming breaths and engage your senses by telling yourself you are about to see, smell, feel, and taste the orange in a new way.

Experience the orange fully. Look at the orange skin and notice its pores. Notice where it is smooth and where it has bumps. Sniff the orange and feel its heft in your hands. Notice what it feels like as you peel or cut the skin. See the inside of the orange with its pith and segments. Bite the orange and let your tongue really experience the tangy sensation. Keep yourself from going on to gobble the orange. Just stay with the experience of appreciating the orange with all of your senses.

Another type of mindfulness practice is walking meditation. In this type of practice, you start by focusing on your environment and then turning inward. Begin by going outside, standing straight, and letting your weight settle, feeling the ground supporting you. Walk and pay attention to the sounds, smells, and sights of the world around you. Also notice your body: the feeling of your heel hitting the ground, your arms swinging, and the breeze touching your skin.

Next, notice what is going on within you. What are you thinking? What are you feeling with your body? Do not judge; just let your mind be what it is and accept it with kindness. After awhile, focus on your breath. Do not force anything; just try to breathe in and out evenly without any "ragged" or catching quality. By focusing on your breath, your mind should begin to quiet down.

As you continue your walk, try shifting your attention between being within your body and paying attention to the environment as you continue to breathe. Accept everything as it is with kindness. If your mind wanders, gently bring it back to the sensations of walking and to what you are experiencing with your senses. When you have completed your walk, bring this feeling of expanded awareness into the next part of your day.

How does all of this mindfulness practice help with sex? As with either of the activities suggested here, when you are involved with sex, you can use your senses to keep you focused on the present moment. Use mindfulness along with the sensate focus activities in appendix 1. Begin by taking turns touching your partner's extremities—the hands, arms, feet, and legs. Pay attention to your partner's skin beneath your fingertips and palms. Listen to their breath, or, if you like, to the music playing as you touch. Notice any odors, without judgment. Gaze into their eyes not just for the sense of sight, but also to strengthen your emotional ties to each other.

As you engage your senses, your mind will quiet down. However, if you do find your mind wandering or experience anxiety, then slowly breathe to calm yourself. You can ask your partner to breathe quietly with you also, perhaps as you hold one another and take a little break from your sensate focus activities.

With practice, the ability to capture that experience of being the only two people in the world, alone and making love, will become easier. However, if you continue to have trouble, you should consider seeing a sex therapist to understand any blocks you have to relaxation.

GLOSSARY

Andropause: A popular term coined to describe the cluster of symptoms that occur as men age, e.g., low mood, irritability, difficulty with erections, etc.

Anorgasmia: The inability to experience orgasm, which can be situational or intermittent; must cause distress to the person.

Arousal: Occurs when the mind and body respond to sexual stimulation.

Cognitive behavioral therapy: A type of psychotherapy that is focused on the current changing of thoughts and behaviors, rather than looking at developmental or past causes of problems.

Delayed ejaculation: Occurs when a man is unable to ejaculate with intercourse or manual stimulation in the presence of his partner. Also used to describe when a man is able to ejaculate only with great effort, up to 30–45 minutes of stimulation.

Dyspareunia: Painful sex, which can be due to problems with internal organs or external genitalia.

Ejaculation: Release of sperm from the male reproductive tract that is usually accompanied by orgasm.

Endocrinologist: Physician who specializes in hormonal balance.

Erectile dysfunction: Diagnosed when a man is unable to attain or sustain an erection firm enough for intercourse.

Erection: Chambers in the penis fill with blood, which enlarges and hardens the penis.

Estrogen: Female hormone that is secreted by the ovaries and is responsible for the development of female sexual characteristics and the menstrual cycle.

Foreplay: Sexual stimulation that leads to arousal and orgasm.

Gynecologist: Physician who specializes in diseases specific to women's reproductive system and sex organs.

Hypersexual: Having a sex drive that most would judge as being stronger than would be expected for a person's given age and circumstance.

Hypertonic pelvic floor muscle: More recent medical term for vaginismus, see below.

Hypoactive sexual desire: Lower desire than is normal for a person's age and stage of life.

Hypomania: Similar to mania, but to a lesser degree. Frequently, it is the spouse or others close to the person with hypomania who notices its symptoms.

Libido: The Latin term for sex drive or appetite.

Mania: Abnormally elevated mood, with such symptoms as inappropriate elation, irritability, sleeplessness, racing thoughts, pressured speech, increased sexual desire, and poor judgment.

Menopause: This stage of a woman's life is attained when menstruation has ceased for 12 months.

Mindfulness: The conscious act of staying focused on the present moment, rather than contemplating the past or present.

Orgasm: A feeling of pleasurable release as a result of sexual stimulation.

Outercourse: Any form of sexual stimulation leading to orgasm that does not involve intercourse, such as oral or manual stimulation.

Oxytocin: The "feel good" chemical released in the brain when people are affectionate or have sex.

Paraphilia: Deviant sexual behavior, such as a shoe fetish or voyeurism.

Performance anxiety: Present when someone feels that their sexual performance is inadequate or they fear being judged by their partner.

Premature ejaculation: When a man ejaculates more quickly than he, or his partner, wants him to, usually in less than three minutes.

Progesterone: Female hormone that along with estrogen is responsible for the regulation of menstruation, pregnancy, and menopause.

Psychosis: Diagnosed when a person loses contact with reality.

Secondary gain: The benefit that someone derives from having an unpleasant condition, e.g., getting attention from a partner.

Selective serotonin reuptake inhibitor (SSRI): A newer type of antidepressant.

Serotonin: A neurotransmitter thought to be responsible for depressed mood when supply is inadequate. Newer antidepressants (SSRIs) are thought to regulate the production of serotonin.

Sexual aversion: Diagnosed when a person has acquired a dislike or disgust of sex.

Sexual dysfunction: Inability to have sexual pleasure due to a psychological or medical problem or both.

Somatoform: A category of mental disorder that involves real and/or imagined physical distress.

Spectatoring: Term coined to describe when a person feels as if they are watching themselves having sex, instead of being in their own body as a participant.

Testosterone: Male hormone produced by the testicles from the start of puberty; responsible for growth and development of male sex and reproductive organs; affects bone mass, fat distribution, muscle, energy levels, sexual desire, penile erection, fertility, and mood. Also present in miniscule amounts in women.

Trigger: An event that triggers an unpleasant physical or emotional memory.

Urologist: Physician who specializes in diseases specific to a man's reproductive system and his sex organs.

Vaginismus: A spasm in the pelvic floor muscle that makes penetration into the vagina painful and/or impossible

Vulvodynia: Painful condition involving the labia and entrance to the vagina.

RESOURCES

Abbey, R. D., J. R. Clopton, and J. D. Humphreys. "Obsessive-Compulsive Disorder and Romantic Functioning." *Journal of Clinical Psychology* 63 (2007): 118–92.

Abdul, Z., R. Thaker, and A. H. Sultan. "Postpartum Female Sexual Function." *European Journal of Obstetrics, Gynecology, & Reproductive Biology* 145 (2009): 133–7.

Abraham, S. "Sexuality and Reproduction in Bulimia Nervosa Patients over 10 Years." *Journal of Psychosomatic Research* 44 (1998): 491–502.

Ackard, D. M., A. Kearney-Cooke, and C. B. Peterson. "Effect of Body Image and Self-Image on Women's Sexual Behaviors." *International Journal of Eating Disorders* 28 (2000): 422–9.

Aksaray, G., Y. Berkant, C. Kaptanoglue, S. Oflu, and M. Ozaltin. "Sexuality in Women with Obsessive-Compulsive Disorder." *Journal of Sex & Marital Therapy* 72 (2001): 273–7.

Atjamasoados, L. "Alcoholism, Marital Problems and Sexual Dysfunction." *Annals of General Hospital Psychiatry* 2, Suppl 1 (2003): S40.

Attwood, T. *The Complete Guide to Asperger's Syndrome.* London: Jessica Kingsley, 2007.

Bahrick, A. S. "Persistence of Sexual Dysfunction Side Effects after Discontinuation of Antidepressant Medications: Emerging Evidence." *The Open Psychiatry Journal* 1 (2008): 42–50.

Baldwin, D. "Depression and Sexual Dysfunction." *British Medical Bulletin* 57 (2001): 88–99.

Baldwin, D., and A. Mayers. "Sexual Side Effects of Antidepressant and Antipsychotic Drugs." *Advances in Psychiatric Treatment* 9 (2003): 202–10.

Balon, R., and R. T. Segraves. "Survey of Treatment Practices for Sexual Dysfunction(s) Associated with Anti-Depressants." *Journal of Sex & Marital Therapy* 34 (2008): 353–65.

Betchen, S. J. "Suggestions for Improving Intimacy in Couples in which One Partner Has Attention-Deficit/Hyperactivity Disorder." *Journal of Sex & Marital Therapy* 29 (2003): 103–24.

Bhui, K., A. Puffet, and G. Strethdee. "Sexual and Relationship Problems amongst Patients with Severe Chronic Psychoses." *Social Psychiatry and Psychiatry Epidemiology* 32 (1997): 459–67.

Blazquez, A., E. Ruiz, T. Vazquez, T. Fernandez de Sevilla, A. Garcia-Quintana, J. Garcia-Quintana, and J. Alegre. "Sexual Dysfunction as Related to Severity of Fatigue in Women with CFS." *Journal of Sex & Marital Therapy* 34 (2008):240–7.

Bouchard, S., S. Sabourin, Y. Lussier, and E. Villeneuve. "Relationship Quality and Stability in Couples When One Partner Suffers from Borderline Personality Disorder." *Journal of Marital and Family Therapy* 35 (2009): 446–55.

Brotto, L. A., M. Basson, and M. Luria. "A Mindfulness-Based Group Psychoeducational Intervention Targeting Sexual Arousal Disorder in Women." *Journal of Sexual Medicine* 5 (2008): 1646–59.

Brunhild, K. "Psychotherapy of Sexual Dysfunction." *American Journal of Psychotherapy* 54 (2000): 97–101.

Chudakov, B., C. Cohen, M. A. Matar, and Z. Kaplan. "A Naturalistic Prospective Open Study of the Effects of Adjunctive Therapy of Sexual Dysfunction in Chronic PTSD Patients." *Israel Journal of Psychiatry & Related Sciences* 45 (2008): 26–32.

Clement, U. "Sex in Long-Term Relationships: A Systemic Approach to Sexual Desire Problems." *Archives of Sexual Behavior* 31 (2002): 241–7.

Cohen, S., K. U. Kuhn, S. Bender, A. Erfurth, M. Gastpar, A. Murafi, M. Rothermundt, et al. "Sexual Impairment in Psychiatric Inpatients: Focus on Depression." *Pharmacopsychiatry* 40 (2007): 58–63.

Conner, M., J. Charlotte, and S. Grogan. "Gender, Sexuality, Body Image, and Eating Behaviors." *Journal of Health Psychology* 9 (2004): 505–15.

Crow, S. J., P. Thuras, P. Keel, and J. E. Mitchell. "Long-Term Menstrual and Reproductive Function in Patients with Bulimia Nervosa." *American Journal of Psychiatry* 159 (2002): 1048–50.

Culbert, K. M., and K. L. Klump. "Impulsivity as an Underlying Factor in the Relationship between Disordered Eating and Sexual Behavior." *International Journal of Eating Disorders* 38 (2005): 361–6.

Cyranowski, J. M., J. Bromberger, A. Youk, K. Matthews, H. M. Kavitz, and L. H. Powell. "Lifetime Depression History and Sexual Function in Women at Midlife." *Archives of Sexual Behavior* 33 (2004): 539–48.

DeLamatar, J., and W. Friedrich. "Human Sexual Development." *The Journal of Sex Research* 39 (2002): 10–14.

De Villers, L., and H. Turgeon. "The Uses and Benefits of "Sensate Focus" Exercises." *Contemporary Sexuality* 39 (2005): i–iv.

Dickerson, F. B., C. H. Brown, J. Kreyenbuhl, R. W. Goldberg, L. J. Fang, and L. B. Dixon. "Sexual and Reproductive Behaviors among Persons with Mental Illness." *Psychiatric Services* 55 (2004): 1299–301.

Duchame, S. "Performance Anxiety." *PN* 63 (2009): 33.

Elliott, A., and T. O'Donohue "The Effects of Anxiety and Distraction on Sexual Arousal in a Nonclinical Sample of Heterosexual Women." *Archives of Sexual Behavior* 26 (1997): 607–25.

Evans, L., and E. H. Wertheim. "Attachment Styles in Adult Intimate Relationships: Comparing Women with Bulimia Nervosa Symptoms, Women with Depression and Women with No Clinical Symptoms." *European Eating Disorders Review* 13 (2005): 285–93.

Fahrner, E. "Sexual Dysfunction in Male Alcohol Addicts: Prevalence and Treatment." *Archives of Sexual Behavior* 16 (1987): 247–57.

Faravelli, C., A. Giugni, S. Salvatori, and V. Ricca. "Psychopathology after Rape." *American Journal of Psychiatry* 161 (2004): 1483–5.

Farina, A., and N. Garmezy. "Relationship of Marital Status to Incidence and Prognosis of Schizophrenia." *Journal of Abnormal and Social Psychology* 67 (1963): 624–30.

Fisher, H. E. *Why We Love: The Nature and Chemistry of Romantic Love*. New York: Henry Holt, 2004.

Foley, S., S. A. Kope, and D. P. Sugrue. *Sex Matters for Women: A Complete Guide for Taking Care of Your Sexual Self*. New York: Guilford Press, 2002.

Fontanelle, L. F., F. Wanderson, G. B. de Menezes, and M. V. Menlowicz. "Sexual Function and Dysfunction in Brazilian Patients with Obsessive-Compulsive Disorder and Social Anxiety Disorder." *Journal of Nervous and Mental Disease* 195 (2007): 254–61.

Foster, J. D., I. Shrira, and W. K. Campbell. "Theoretical Models of Narcissism, Sexuality, and Relationship Commitment." *Journal of Social and Personal Relationships* 23 (2006): 367–86.

Grant, J. E., A. Pinto, M. Gunnip, M. C. Mancebo, J. L. Eisen, and S. A. Rasmussen. "Sexual Obsessions and Clinical Correlates in Adults with Obsessive-Compulsive Disorder." *Comprehensive Psychiatry* 47 (2006): 325–9.

Hall, J. H., W. Fals-Stewart, and F. D. Fincham. "Risky Sexual Behavior among Married Alcoholic Men." *Journal of Family Psychology* 22 (2008): 287–92.

Hall, K. "Childhood Sexual Abuse and Adult Sexual Problems: A New View of Assessment and Treatment." *Feminism & Psychology* 18 (2008): 546–56.

Halverstadt, J. *A.D.D. and Romance*. Lanham, MA: Taylor Trade Publishing, 1998.

Hickey, D., A. Carr, B. Dooley, S. Guerin, E. Butler, and L. Fitzpatrick, L. "Family and Marital Profiles of Couples in which One Partner Has Depression or Anxiety." *Journal of Marital and Family Therapy* 31 (2005): 171–82.

Hicks, T. L., S. F. Goodall, E. M. Quattrone, M. T. Lydon-Rochelle. "Postpartum Sexual Functioning and Method of Delivery: Summary of the Evidence." *Journal of Midwifery & Women's Health* 49 (2004): 430–6.

Higgins, A., P. Barker, and C. M. Begley. "Neuroleptic Medication and Sexuality: The Forgotten Aspect of Education and Care." *Journal of Psychiatric and Mental Health Nursing* 12 (2005): 439–46.

Higgins, A., P. Barker, and C. M. Begley. "Sexual Health Education for People with Mental Health Problems: What Can We Learn from the Literature?" *Journal of Psychiatric and Mental Health Nursing* 13 (2005): 687–97.

James, R. "Strategies for Incorporating Women-Specific Sexuality Education into Addiction Treatment Models." *American Journal of Sexuality Education* 2 (2007): 3–25.

Joannides, P. *Guide to Getting It On: For Adults of All Ages*. Waldport, OR: Goofyfoot Press, 2009.

Johnson, S. D., D. L. Phelps, and L. B. Cottler. "The Association of Sexual Dysfunction and Substance Use among a Community Epidemiological Sample." *Archives of Sexual Behavior* 33 (2004): 55–63.

Kabat-Zinn, J. "Mindfulness-Based Interventions in Context: Past, Present, and Future." *Clinical Psychology: Science and Practice* 10 (2003): 144–56.

Kalichman, L. "Association between Fibromyalgia and Sexual Dysfunction in Women." *Clinical Rheumatology* 28 (2009): 365–9.

Katz, A. *Sex When You're Sick: Reclaiming Sexual Health after Illness or Injury*. Westport, CT: Praeger Publishers, 2007.

Kender, K. S., J. Kuhn, and C. A. Prescott. "The Interrelationship of Neuroticism, Sex, and Stressful Life Events in the Prediction of Episodes of Major Depression." *The American Journal of Psychiatry* 161 (2004): 631–7.

Kendurkar, A., and K. Brinder. "Major Depressive Disorder, Obsessive-Compulsive Disorder, and Generalized Anxiety Disorder: Do the Sexual Dysfunctions Differ?" *Primary Care Companion to the Journal of Clinical Psychiatry* 10 (2008): 299–305.

La Pera, G., A. Carderi, M. Zelinda, F. Peris, M. Lentini, and F. Taggi. "Sexual Dysfunction Prior to First Drug Use among Former Drug Addicts and Its Possible Causal Meaning on Drug Addiction: Preliminary Results." *Journal of Sexual Medicine* 5 (2008): 164–72.

Leiblum, S. R. *Principles and Practice of Sex Therapy.* New York: Guilford Press, 2007.

Lester, R. J. "The (Dis)Embodied Self in Anorexia Nervosa." *Social Science & Medicine* 44 (1997): 479–89.

Lew, M. *Victims No Longer: The Classic Guide for Men Recovering from Sexual Child Abuse.* New York: Quill, 2004.

Liebschultz, J., J. B. Savetsky, R. Saitz, N. J. Horton, C. Lloyd-Travaglini, and J. H. Samet. "The Relationship between Sexual and Physical Abuse and Substance Abuse Consequences." *Journal of Substance Abuse Treatment* 22 (2002): 121–8.

Mallis, D., M. Kyriakos, E. Nakopoulou, S. Papaharitou, K. Hatzimouratidis, and D. Hatzichristou. "Psychiatric Morbidity is Frequently Undetected in Patients with Erectile Dysfunction." *The Journal of Urology* 174 (2005): 1913–6.

McCabe, M. P. "The Interrelationship between Intimacy, Relationship Functioning, and Sexuality among Men and Women in Committed Relationships." *The Canadian Journal of Human Sexuality* 8 (1999): 31–38.

McCandless, F., and C. Sladen. "Sexual Health and Women with Bipolar Disorder." *Journal of Advanced Nursing* 44 (2003): 42–8.

McCann, E. "The Expression of Sexuality in People with Psychosis: Breaking the Taboos." *Journal of Psychiatric and Mental Health Nursing* 32 (2000): 132–8.

McCann, E. "Exploring Sexual and Relationship Possibilities for People with Psychosis— A Review of the Literature." *Journal of Psychiatric and Mental Health Nursing* 10 (2003): 640–9.

McCann, E. "Investigating Mental Health Service User Views Regarding Sexual and Relationship Issues." *Journal of Psychiatric and Mental Health Nursing* 17 (2010): 251–9.

Medley, I., and A. R. Douglas. "Sexuality and Mental Illness: A Small Group Approach." *Bulletin of the Royal College of Psychiatrists* 12 (1998): 132–134.

Metz, M. E., and B. W. McCarthy. *Coping with Erectile Dysfunction: How to Regain Confidence and Enjoy Great Sex.* Oakland, CA: New Harbinger Publications, 2004.

Michetti, P. M., R. Rossi, D. Bonanno, A. Tiesi, and C. Simonelli. "Male Sexuality and Regulation of Emotions: A Study on the Association between Alexithymia and Erectile Dysfunction (ED)." *International Journal of Impotence Research* 18 (2006): 170–4.

Millon, M., C. M. Millon, S. Meagher, S. Grossman, and R. Ramnath. *Personality Disorders in Modern Life,* 2nd ed. Hoboken, NJ: Wiley, 2004.

Monga, T. N., G. Tan, H. J. Ostermann, U. Monga, and M. Grabois, M. "Sexuality and Sexual Adjustment of Patients with Chronic Pain." *Disability Rehabilitation* 20 (1998): 317–29.

Nhat Hanh, T. *The Miracle of Mindfulness: An Introduction to the Practice of Meditation.* Boston: Beacon Press, 1999.

Nicolosi, A., E. D. Moreira, M. Villa, and D. B. Glasser. "A Population Study of the Association between Sexual Function, Sexual Satisfaction and Depressive Symptoms in Men." *Journal of Affective Disorders* 82 (2004): 235–43.

Palha, A. "Drugs and Sexuality." *Sexologies* 17 (2008): S1–2.

Pearlman, J. "Hypochondria: The Impossible Illness." *Psychology Today* Jan/Feb (2010).

Pirard, S., E. Sharon, S. K. Kang, G. A. Angarita, D. R. Gastfriend. "Prevalence of Physical and Sexual Abuse among Substance Abuse Patients and Impact on Treatment Outcomes." *Drug and Alcohol Dependence* 78 (2005): 57–64.

Quadflieg, N., and M. F. Manfred. "The Course and Outcome of Bulimia Nervosa." *European Child & Adolescent Psychiatry* 12, Suppl 1 (2003): 99–109.

Randolph, M. E., and D. M. Reddy. "Sexual Abuse and Sexual Functioning in a Chronic Pelvic Pain Sample." *Journal of Child Sexual Abuse* 15 (2006): 61–8.

Reise, S. P., and T. M. Wright. "Brief Report: Personality Traits, Cluster B Personality Disorders, and Sociosexuality." *Journal of Research in Personality* 30 (1996): 128–36.

Rodriquez, S., J. L. Mata, M. Lameiras, M. C. Fernandez, and J. Vila. "Dyscontrol Evoked by Erotic and Food Images in Women with Bulimia Nervosa." *European Eating Disorders Review* 15 (2007): 231–9.

Rosen, R., R. Shabsigh, M. Berber, P. Assalian, M. Menza, L. Rodriguez-Vela, R. Porto, et al. "Efficacy and Tolerability of Vardenafil in Men with Mild Depression and Erectile Dysfunction: The Depression-Related Improvement with Vardenafil for Erectile Response Study." *American Journal of Psychiatry* 163 (2006): 78–87.

Sachs-Ericsson, N., K. Cromer, A. Hernandez, and K. Kendall-Tackett. "A Review of Childhood Abuse, Health, and Pain-Related Problems: The Role of Psychiatric Disorders and Current Life Stress." *Journal of Trauma and Dissociation* 10 (2009): 170–88.

Sanchez, D. T., and A. K. Kiefer. "Body Concerns in and out of the Bedroom: Implications for Sexual Pleasure and Problems." *Archives of Sexual Behavior* 36 (2007): 808–20.

Shafer, A. "The Big Five and Sexuality Trait Terms as Predictors of Relationships and Sex." *Journal of Research in Personality* 35 (2001): 313–38.

Sobsczak, J. A. "Struggling to Reconnect: Women's Perspectives on Alcohol Dependence, Violence, and Sexual Function." *Journal of the American Psychiatric Nurses Association* 14 (2009): 421–8.

South, S. C., E. Turkheimer, and T. F. Oltmanns. "Personality Disorder Symptoms and Marital Functioning." *Journal of Consulting and Clinical Psychology* 76 (2008): 769–80.

Sperry, L., and J. Carlson. "Couples Therapy with a Personality-Disordered Couple." *The Family Journal: Counseling and Therapy for Couples and Families* 8 (2000): 118–23.

Stanford, A. *Asperger Syndrome and Long-Term Relationships.* London: Jessica Kingsley, 2003.

Stewart, S. E., D. E. Stack, and S. Wilhelm, S. "Severe Obsessive-Compulsive Disorder with and without Body Dysmorphic Disorder: Clinical Correlates and Implications." *Journal of Clinical Psychiatry* 201 (2008): 33–8.

Turner, D. S., and F. A. Dudek. "An Analysis of Alcoholism and Its Effects on Sexual Functioning." *Sexuality and Disability* 5 (1982): 143–57.

Van Minnen, A., and M. Kampman. "The Interaction between Anxiety and Sexual Functioning: A Controlled Study of Sexual Functioning in Women with Anxiety Disorders." *Sexual and Relationship Therapy* 15 (2000): 47–57.

Wiederman, M. W. "Women, Sex, and Food: A Review of Research on Eating Disorders and Sexuality." *The Journal of Sex Research* 33 (1996): 301–11.

Wiederman, M. W., and T. Pryor. "Body Dissatisfaction and Sexuality among Women with Bulimia Nervosa." *International Journal of Eating Disorders* 21 (1997): 361–5.

Wiederman, M. W., and T. Pryor. "Body Dissatisfaction, Bulimia, and Depression among Women: The Mediating Role of Drive for Thinness." *International Journal of Eating Disorders* 27 (2000): 90–95.

Wiederman, M. W., and R. A. Sansone. "Borderline Personality Disorder and Sexuality." *The Family Journal: Counseling and Therapy for Couples and Families* 17 (2009): 277–82.

Williams, T. L., and D. H. Gleaves. "Childhood Sexual Abuse, Body Image, and Disordered Eating: A Structural Modeling Analysis." *Journal of Trauma and Dissociation* 4 (2003): 91–108.

Zakhari, R. "Female Sexual Dysfunction: A Primary Care Perspective." *Journal of the American Academy of Nurse Practitioners* 21 (2009): 498–505.

INDEX

About the Author and Series Editor

STEPHANIE BUEHLER, MPW, PsyD, is director of The Buehler Institute in Irvine, California, and an internationally recognized psychologist and sex therapist. Dr. Buehler is the author of *Sex & Passion: The Essential Guide, Now and Forever*, former editor of the *Women's Sexual Health Journal*, and an active blogger on the topic of sexuality. She has been featured in the popular media, including *Esquire, Time, Woman's Day*, and many others.

JUDY KURIANSKY, PhD, is an internationally known, licensed Clinical Psychologist and an adjunct faculty member in the Department of Clinical Psychology at Columbia University Teachers College and in the Department of Psychiatry at Columbia University College of Physicians and Surgeons. At the United Nations, she is an NGO representative for the International Association of Applied Psychology and for the World Council for Psychotherapy, and is an executive member of the Committee of Mental Health. She is also a Visiting Professor at the Peking University Health Sciences Center, a Fellow of the American Psychological Association, cofounder of the APA Media Psychology Division, and on the board of the Peace Division and U.S. Doctors for Africa. A certified sex therapist by the American Association of Sex Educators and Counselors, she is a pioneer in the field of sexuality. An award-winning journalist, she hosted the popular LovePhones syndicated call-in radio show for years, was a feature reporter for WCBS-TV and CNBC, and regularly comments on news and current events on television worldwide. Her wide-ranging expertise in interpersonal and international relations is evident in her books ranging from *The Complete Idiot's Guide to a Healthy Relationship* and *Sexuality Education: Past, Present and Future* to *Beyond Bullets and Bombs: Grassroots Peacebuilding between Israelis and Palestinians*. Her website is www .DrJudy.com.